Scott, Foresman **Spelling**

train

Authors

Linda Ward Beech
James Beers
Ronald L. Cramer
W. Dorsey Hammond
Lida F. Lim
Patricia Muncy
John Prejza, Jr.
DeWayne Triplett

Scott, Foresman and Company

Editorial Offices:
Glenview, Illinois

Regional Offices:
Sunnyvale, California
Tucker, Georgia
Glenview, Illinois
Oakland, New Jersey
Dallas, Texas

Acknowledgments

Text

page 36: From EASY DOES IT! *Things to Make and Do* by James Razzi. Copyright © 1969 by James Razzi. Reprinted by permission of Scholastic Inc.
page 88: From THE PATCHWORK QUILT by Valerie Flournoy. New York: Dial Books for Young Readers, 1985.
page 114: From DEAR PHOEBE by Sue Alexander. Copyright © 1984 by Sue Alexander. Reprinted by permission of Little, Brown and Company and Curtis Brown, Ltd.
page 166: Excerpt and illustration from THE BREMEN-TOWN MUSICIANS by Ilse Plume. Copyright © 1980 by Ilse Plume. Reprinted by permission of Doubleday & Company, Inc.
page 175: From "Fitzgerald's Master Demon List of 222 Words." Reprinted, with permission, from The American School Board Journal, July 1941, Copyright 1941, the National School Boards Association. All rights reserved.
page 175: From "One Hundred Words Most Often Misspelled by Children in the Elementary Grades" by Leslie W. Johnson, JOURNAL OF EDUCATIONAL RESEARCH, 44: 154-155
page 175: From CONCRETE INVESTIGATION OF THE MATERIAL OF ENGLISH SPELLING by W. Franklin Jones. Copyright 1913 University of South Dakota. Reprinted by permission of the University of South Dakota.
page 175: From "Misspelling in Grades 9-12" by Thomas Clark Pollock, ENGLISH RECORD, Vol. 22, No. 1, Fall 1971. Copyright © 1971 by the New York State English Council. Reprinted by permission.

Illustrations

Section 1: Robert Masheris
Section 2: Lydia Halverson
Section 3: Dennis Hockerman
Section 4: Dick Martin
Section 5: Margaret Sanfilippo
Section 6: Nan Brooks
Word Building/Word Study: Eileen Mueller Neill
Spelling Strategies: James Higa
Reviews: Don Charles
pages 63, 115: Tom McKee

Photographs

Cover: Ann & Myron Sutton/FPG
Word Building/Word Study: James L. Ballard
Len Bouche 250T; Chan Bush 253; Joseph A. DiChello 231T, 236T, 236B, 239B, 240T, 242B, 245, 246B, 247, 249, 251, 258, 264T, 268T, 272T, 272C, 272B Cy Furlan 233T, 234B, NASA 232T; Art Pahlke 231B, 232B, 233B, 239T, 240B, 243, 244B, 248, 256, 257, 259, 261, 262T, 263, 264B, 267, 268B, 269, 271, 276T, 277, 278T; Chuck Rydlewski 235G, 244T, 254T, 255, 266B, 275T; Don and Pat Valenti 234T, 238, 242T, 246T, 252, 254B, 265, 266T, 276B, 279, 280T
All photographs not specifically credited are Scott, Foresman photographs.

ISBN 0-673-27704-6

Printed in the United States of America.

345678910-VHJ-9695949392919089887

Contents

How to Study a Word

1. Look at the word. Say it and listen to its sounds.
2. Say the letters in order.
3. Close your eyes and recall the letters.
4. Write the word while looking at it.
5. Cover the word and write it. Check to see if you spelled it correctly. If not, repeat the steps.
6. Write the word correctly two more times.

Starting a Spelling Notebook

Setting up a spelling notebook is easy. Divide your notebook into two parts. The first part can be for words you use often in writing.

1. Use one page for each letter of the alphabet.
2. Write the word under the correct letter.
3. Write the meaning of the word.
4. Use the word in a sentence.

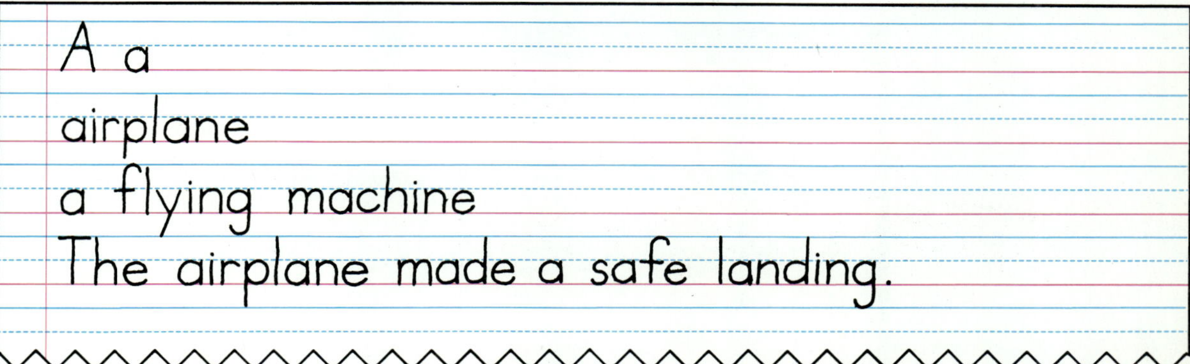

Use the second part of your notebook for assignments and activities from your spelling book.

1. Write words you misspell on the pretest.
2. Complete homework assignments.
3. Write your own list of difficult words.

Lesson 1	Homework Assignments
Pretest	Practice the Words:
have	Rhyming
dad	can
Difficult Words	man
pat	ran
have	

Introduction

Words with Short a

Focus These words have the **short a** sound in **cat**.

- **Short a** may be spelled **a**.

Say the Words

Listen for the **short a** sound.

1. dad	7. bad
2. had	8. sat
3. pat	9. tag
4. can	10. man
5. has	11. ran
6. have	12. half

Wild Words The words *have* and *half* begin with the letter **h** and have the **short a** sound. However, they end in a different way. Notice how each word is spelled.

Practice the Words

1. Write the words that rhyme with *sad*.
2. Write the words that begin or end with **t**.
3. Write the word that ends like *his*.
4. Write the words that rhyme with *van*.
5. Write the words with four letters.

Sum Up What did you learn about how **short a** may be spelled?

More Practice

For Extra Practice, see page 188.

Change one letter to make a list word. Write the word.

1. pot
2. cat
3. did
4. hive
5. hid
6. his

Write the list word to finish each sentence.

7. I ate ___ of my sandwich.
8. Who is that ___?
9. Let's play ___.
10. The dog ___ fast.
11. We ___ on the sofa.
12. I had a ___ cold.

Word Building

Listen for the **-at** in **pat**. Add **-at** to make a new word.

1. m ___ 2. fl ___ 3. th ___

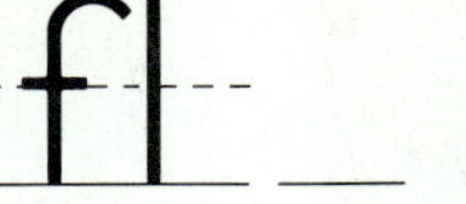

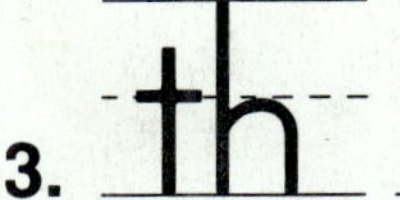

Listen for the **-ad** in **dad**. Add **-ad** to make a new word.

1. m ___ 2. p ___ 3. gl ___

Spelling Connections

dad
had
pat
can
has
have

bad
sat
tag
man
ran
half

Spelling and Language Skills

Statements A **sentence** is a group of words that tells a complete idea. A **statement** is a sentence that tells something. A statement begins with a **capital letter** and ends with a **period** [.].

The man cannot find his cat.

Proofreading Write each sentence correctly. Check for capital letters, periods, and correct spelling.

1. we hav a dog
2. it ren after the cat

Spelling and Handwriting Skills

Write **a** and **h**. The **a** starts at the middle line. The **h** starts at the top line. Write *has*.

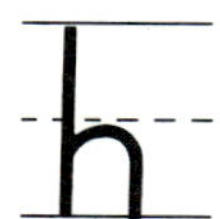

Spelling and Writing

What did these animals do? Write three sentences about it. Use list words such as *ran*, *can*, and *bad*. Revise and proofread your sentences.

Review and Extend

Checkup

Write a list word by adding the missing letter or letters.

1. h_v_	4. p_t
2. d_d	5. h_s
3. c_n	6. h_d

7. h_lf	10. t_g
8. b_d	11. r_n
9. s_t	12. m_n

Bonus Words

an
am
at
a

Write the bonus word to finish each sentence.

1. I have ___ apple.
2. I got it ___ the store.
3. Do you want ___ bite?
4. Yes, I ___ hungry.

Challenge Words Health

banana
sandwich
milk
potatoes
stew

Write the word for each meaning.

1. vegetables that grow underground
2. yellow fruit
3. a drink that comes from a cow
4. pieces of bread with food between them
5. meat and vegetables cooked together

2 Words with Short e

Introduction

Focus These words have the **short e** sound in **pen**.

- **Short e** may be spelled **e**.

Say the Words

Listen for the **short e** sound.

1. ten	7. met
2. men	8. let
3. get	9. set
4. red	10. hen
5. yes	11. pen
6. said	12. seven

Wild Words The words *said* and *seven* have the **short e** sound. Notice how each is spelled.

Practice the Words

1. Write the words that end like *cat*.
2. Write the words that end like *pin*.
3. Write the word that begins like *yellow*.
4. Write the words that rhyme with *bed*.

Sum Up What did you learn about how **short e** may be spelled?

More Practice

For Extra Practice, see page 189.

Write the list word that fits into each word shape.

1. 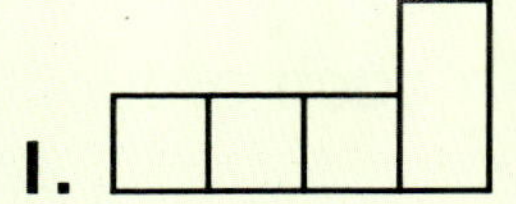
2. 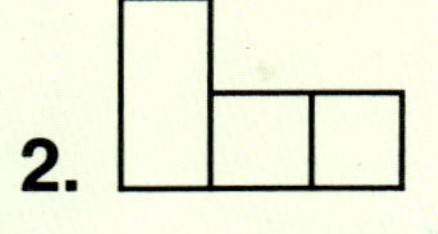
3. 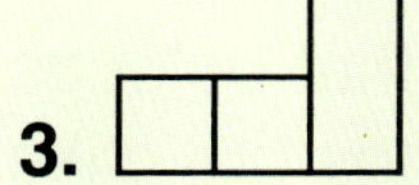
4. 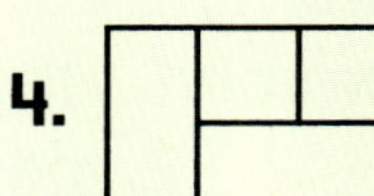
5. 
6.

Write the list word to finish each sentence.

Ted and I (7) at the zoo. We saw (8) seals. The zoo keeper (9) us feed them.

We have a pet (10). Dad and I built a (11) for it. We (12) it up in the backyard.

Word Building

Listen for the **-et** in **get**. Add **-et** to make a new word.

1. 
2. 
3. 

Listen for the **-ed** in **red**. Add **-ed** to make a new word.

1. 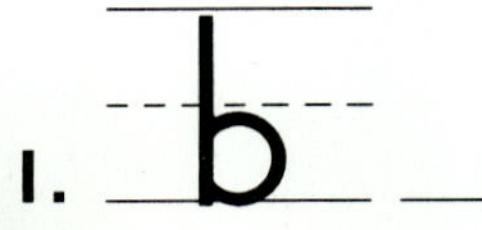
2. 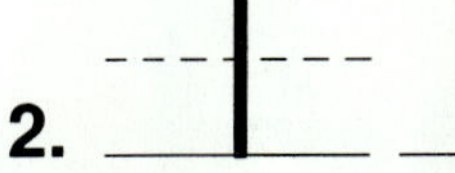
3. 

2 Application

ten
men
get
red
yes
said

met
let
set
hen
pen
seven

Spelling Connections

Spelling and Thinking Skills

Comparing You can compare things to see how they are alike.

Write the list word that belongs with each group. Then tell how the things are alike.

Example: children, women, ___

Answer: children, women, men

1. two, five, ___
2. pencil, crayon, ___

Spelling and Dictionary Skills

Alphabetizing The letters below are in alphabetical order.

a b c d e f g h i j k l m n o p q r s t u v w x y z

Write the letters in alphabetical order.

1. i g h
2. n p o m l
3. r q p s
4. z y w v u x

Spelling and Writing

Write three sentences about this animal. Use list words such as *get*, *ten*, and *let*. Revise and proofread your sentences.

Review and Extend

Checkup

Write a list word by adding the missing letter or letters.

1. y_s_	4. s__d	7. s_v_n	10. p_n
2. t_n	5. r_d	8. m_t	11. h_n
3. g_t	6. m_n	9. s_t	12. l_t

Bonus Words

bed
pet
wet

Write the bonus word to finish each sentence.

1. A family animal is called a ___.
2. A place to sleep is called a ___.
3. When it rains, you can get ___.

Challenge Words Mathematics

trade
sell
cents
change
borrow

Write the word for each meaning.

1. pennies
2. to use and return
3. to exchange for another
4. to make different
5. to give for money

3 Words with Short i

Introduction

Focus These words have the **short i** sound in **pin**.
- **Short i** may be spelled **i**.

Say the Words

Listen for the **short i** sound.

1. his	7. sit
2. did	8. bit
3. six	9. tip
4. him	10. dig
5. if	11. big
6. give	12. been

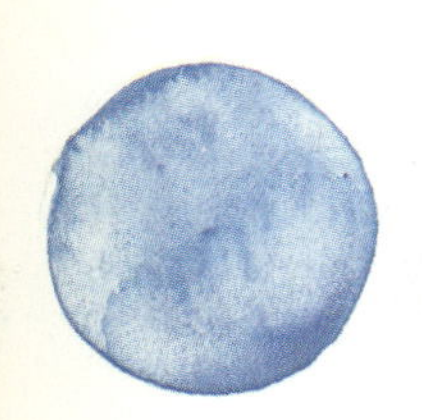

Wild Words The words *give* and *been* have a **short i** sound. Notice how the **short i** sound is spelled in each word.

Practice the Words

1. Write the words starting with letters **a** to **f**.
2. Write the words starting with letters **g** to **l**.
3. Write the words starting with letters **m** to **t**.

Sum Up What did you learn about how **short i** may be spelled?

 For Extra Practice, see page 190.

Write the list word to finish each sentence.

1. The game starts at ___.
2. Ask dad ___ we can go.
3. What ___ he say?
4. Will he ___ us a ride?
5. I'll ask ___ now.
6. Dad can't find ___ keys.

Write the list word to complete each phrase.

7. just a little ___
8. ___ of your nose
9. ___ in a chair
10. a ___ apple
11. never ___ happier
12. ___ with a shovel

Word Building

Listen for the **-id** in **did**. Add **-id** to make a new word.

1. l ___
2. sk ___
3. sl ___

Listen for the **-im** in **him**. Add **-im** to make a new word.

4. d ___
5. tr ___
6. sw ___

3 Application

Spelling Connections

his
did
six
him
if
give

sit
bit
tip
dig
big
been

Spelling and Language Skills

Questions A **question** is a sentence that asks something. A question begins with a **capital letter** and ends with a **question mark** [?].

What time is it?

Proofreading Write each sentence correctly. Check for capital letters, question marks, and spelling.

1. what did he giv you
2. where has he bin

Spelling and Handwriting Skills

Write **f** and **t**. The **f** starts below the top line. The **t** starts near the top line. Remember to cross the **f** and **t**. Then write *if* and *it*.

Spelling and Writing

Write three questions you might ask about a walk along a nature trail. Use list words such as *big*, *did*, and *been*. Revise and proofread your sentences.

Review and Extend

Checkup

Write a list word by adding the missing letter or letters.

1. g_v_	4. _f	7. b_g	10. b__n
2. h_m	5. h_s	8. t_p	11. d_g
3. s_x	6. d_d	9. s_t	12. b_t

Bonus Words

it
in
is

Write the bonus word to finish each sentence.

1. Where ___ the ball?
2. Tom says ___ isn't here.
3. It must be ___ the house.

Challenge Words Science

stem
plants
leaf
petal
dandelion

Write the word to finish each sentence.

1. Tulips and corn are two kinds of ___.
2. That tree has a beautiful red ___.
3. I pulled up the ___. It is a weed.
4. The bee landed on the ___ of the rose.
5. The hard rain bent the ___ of that plant.

4 Words with Short o

Introduction

Focus These words have the **short o** sound in **pot**.

- **Short o** may be spelled **o**.

Say the Words

Listen for the **short o** sound.

1. got	7. job
2. lot	8. top
3. hot	9. hop
4. box	10. spot
5. mom	11. doll
6. gone	12. upon

Wild Words The word *gone* does not have a **short o** sound. The vowel sound is /ô/. The words *up* and *on* make up the word *upon*.

Practice the Words

1. Write the words that rhyme with *dot*.
2. Write the words that begin or end with **b**.
3. Write the word that ends like *drum*.
4. Write the words with *on* in them.
5. Write the words from 7 to 12 that rhyme.
6. Write the word that begins with **d**.

Sum Up How may **short o** be spelled?

Review and Extend

Checkup

Write a list word by adding the missing letters.

1. __x	4. ___e	7. ___n	10. t__
2. h__	5. l__	8. j__	11. sp__
3. __m	6. g__	9. d__	12. h__

Bonus Words

on
not
of

Write the bonus word to finish each sentence.

1. There is ____ enough milk.
2. Do you want a glass ____ juice?
3. It is ____ the top shelf.

Challenge Words Social Studies

doctor
printer
firefighter
baker
pilot

Write the word to answer each question.

1. Who puts out fires?
2. Who flies a plane?
3. Who helps us when we're sick?
4. Who makes bread and rolls?
5. Who produces books and newspapers?

5 Words with Short u

Introduction

Focus These words have the **short u** sound in **cup**.
- **Short u** may be spelled **u**.

Say the Words

Listen for the **short u** sound.

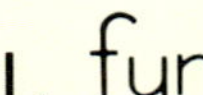

1. fun
2. run
3. sun
4. but
5. bug
6. was
7. bus
8. gum
9. mud
10. rug
11. nut
12. once

Wild Words The words *was* and *once* have the **short u** sound. Notice how the **short u** sound is spelled in each.

Practice the Words

1. Write the words from 1 to 6 that rhyme.
2. Write the words from 1 to 6 that begin like *box*.
3. Write the word that rhymes with *buzz*.
4. Write the words from 7 to 12 in alphabetical order.

Sum Up What did you learn about how **short u** may be spelled?

For Extra Practice, see page 192.

Read the clues. Then write the list words.

1. I begin with **s**.
2. I begin with **f**.
3. I end with **s**.
4. I end with **g**.
5. I begin with **r**.
6. I end with **t**.

Write the list word for each clue. The letters in the box answer the riddle.

7. way to travel
8. inside a shell
9. near your teeth
10. very wet dirt
11. one time
12. covering for the floor

7. ___ ___ ___
8. ___ ___ ___
9. ___ ___ ___
10. ___ ___ ___
11. ___ ___ ___ ___
12. ___ ___ ___

I follow spring. What am I? ___

Word Building

Listen for the **-ug** in **bug**. Add **-ug** to make a new word.

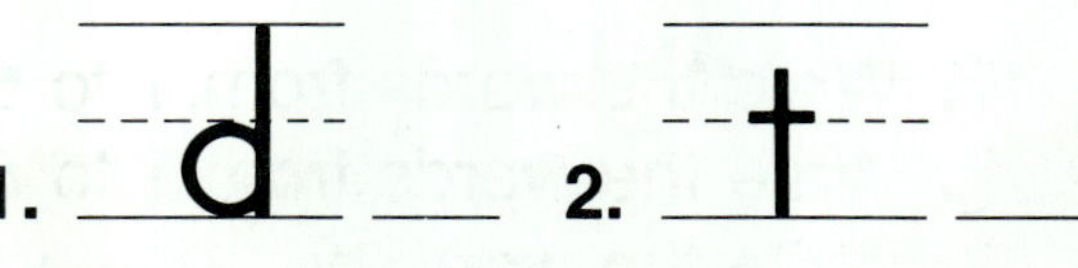

1. d ___ 2. t ___ 3. pl ___

Listen for the **-ut** in **but**. Add **-ut** to make a new word.

1. h ___ 2. c ___ 3. sh ___

fun
run
sun
but
bug
was

bus
gum
mud
rug
nut
once

Spelling Connections

Spelling and Language Skills

Capitalization and End Punctuation All sentences begin with a **capital letter**. A **statement** ends with a **period** [.]. A **question** ends with a **question mark** [?].

We went to the lake.

Did you have fun?

Proofreading Write each sentence correctly. Check for capital letters, periods, question marks, and spelling.

1. did you ron fast
2. we had to catch the buse

Spelling and Handwriting Skills

Write **b** and **c**. The **b** starts at the top line. The **c** starts just below the middle line. Then write *bug* and *once*.

Spelling and Writing

What do you like best in this picture? Write three sentences about it. Use list words such as *fun*, *sun*, and *was*. Revise and proofread your sentences.

Review and Extend

Checkup

Write a list word by adding the missing letter.

1. w_s	4. s_n
2. b_g	5. b_t
3. r_n	6. f_n

7. _nce	10. n_t
8. m_d	11. g_m
9. b_s	12. r_g

Bonus Words

us
up
hug
rub

Write the bonus word that fits into each word shape.

1. 2. 3. 4.

Challenge Words Science

lion
llama
cougar
buffalo
giraffe

Write the words to finish the story.

Dear Diary,

I want to work in a zoo. I'd brush the mane of a __(1)__. I would use a ladder to feed a __(2)__. What fun to pet a wooly-haired __(3)__! I would keep away from the long horns of the water __(4)__. I'd feed the __(5)__ huge pieces of meat. I'd be a great zoo writer.

6 Review

Spelling Strategy

Making a Spelling Notebook Make one page for each letter of the alphabet. Follow these steps to add a word to your notebook. First, write the word. Next, write its meaning. Last, write the word in a sentence. Here is an example:

said spoke *Jack said the word carefully.*

Activity Make your own spelling notebook. Choose three words from Lessons 1 to 5 for your notebook.

Words with Short a Words with the **short a** sound in **cat** may be spelled with an **a**.

Write each group of words. Then circle the letter that makes the **short a** sound.

1

dad **had** **pat** **can** **has** **have**

1. ___
2. ___
3. ___
4. ___
5. ___
6. ___

bad **sat** **tag** **man** **ran** **half**

7. ___
8. ___
9. ___
10. ___
11. ___
12. ___

Words with Short e Words with the **short e** sound in **pen** may be spelled with an **e**.

2

ten **men** **get** **red** **yes** **said**

Change the vowel in each word to make a list word with the **short e** sound.

1. got ___ **3. man** ___
2. tan ___ **4. rod** ___

Write the list words in alphabetical order. Then circle the letter or letters that make the **short e** sound in each word.

1. ___ **4.** ___
2. ___ **5.** ___
3. ___ **6.** ___

met **let** **set** **hen** **pen** **seven**

Write the words in alphabetical order. Underline the letter that makes the **short e** sound in each word.

7. ___ **10.** ___
8. ___ **11.** ___
9. ___ **12.** ___

Words with Short i Words with the **short i** sound in **pi̲n** may be spelled with an **i**.

Write each group of words. Then circle the letter or letters that make the **short i** sound in each word.

3

his **did** **six** **him** **if** **give**

1. ___
2. ___
3. ___
4. ___
5. ___
6. ___

sit **bit** **tip** **dig** **big** **been**

7. ___
8. ___
9. ___
10. ___
11. ___
12. ___

Words with Short o Words with the **short o** sound in **po̲t** may be spelled **o**.

Write a list word by adding the missing letter that makes the **short o** sound.

4

got **hot** **mom**
lot **box** **gone**

1. b_x
2. m_m
3. l_t
4. g_ne
5. h_t
6. g_t

job **hop** **doll**
top **spot** **upon**

7. h_p
8. sp_t
9. d_ll
10. up_n
11. j_b
12. t_p

Words with Short u Words with the **short u** sound in **c<u>u</u>p** may be spelled with a **u**.

5

Write the words. Underline the letter that makes the **short u** sound in each word.

fun **run** **sun** **but** **bug** **was**

1. ___ **3.** ___ **5.** ___
2. ___ **4.** ___ **6.** ___

Write the list word that does not have **short u** spelled **u**. **6a.** ___

bus **gum** **mud** **rug** **nut** **once**

Write each word below. Then underline in it the list word with the **short u** sound.

muddle rugged gummy bustle nutty

7. ___ **9.** ___ **11.** ___
8. ___ **10.** ___

Write the list word that does not have **short u** spelled **u**. **12.** ___

Spelling Connections

Reading Directions

In this lesson, you will make two nighttime animals—a mouse and a porcupine. You will write directions for making the porcupine.

Read the directions for making the mouse. The words *first*, *next*, *then*, and *last* show the order of the steps.

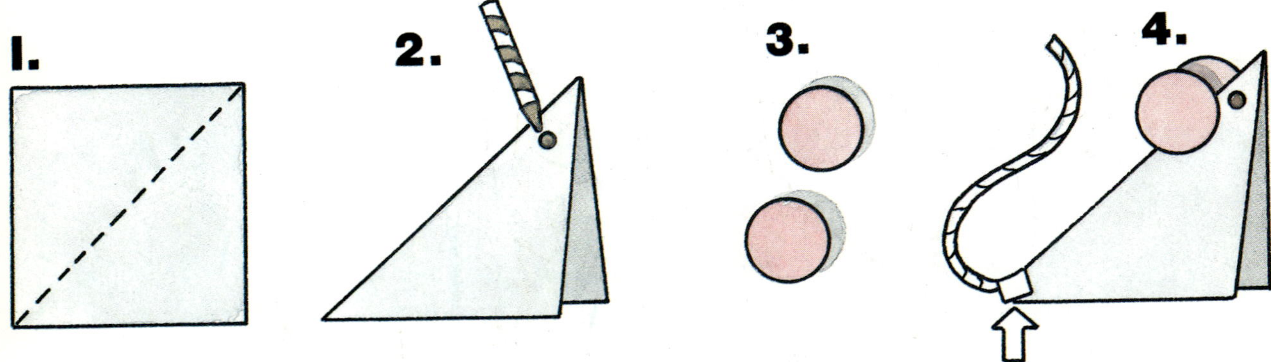

First, cut out a piece of paper, four inches square. Fold it as shown in pictures 1 and 2. **Next,** draw two small dots for the eyes, one on each side of the fold as in picture 2. **Then,** cut out two small circles, about as big as bottle caps. See picture 3. These will be the ears. Paste one circle on each side of the fold just behind the eyes. See figure 4. **Last,** tape or paste a piece of string for the mouse's tail as shown in picture 4.

from *Easy Does It!* by James Razzi

Answer the questions.

1. Which part of the mouse is made first?
2. What parts are added later?

Speaking and Listening

Work with a classmate. Talk about what you do in each step of the directions. Then make the mouse together.

Writing Directions

Now you will write directions for making the porcupine. Write your directions so that a first-grader can use them. Follow the steps below.

Prewriting Study the pictures to find out what is done in each step.

Writing Write what you do in each step. Use the words *first*, *next*, *then*, and *last* to show the order of the steps. Use words from the review box.

Revising Read over your directions. Be sure you used the words *first*, *next*, *then*, and *last*. Check your spelling of the review words. Use the checklists on pages 176 and 177.

Presenting Read your directions to a first-grader. Make a porcupine together. Let the first-grader keep the directions.

Review Words

pat
can
has
have
get
his
him
give
got
but

7 Words with c, k, and ck

Introduction

Focus These words have the consonant sound /k/ in **car, kite,** and **black**. This consonant sound may be spelled **c, k,** and **ck**.

Say the Words

Listen for the consonant sound /k/.

1. cup
2. kid
3. back
4. duck
5. sock
6. kitten
7. neck
8. kick
9. sick
10. pick
11. rock
12. picnic

Wild Words The words *kitten* and *picnic* have the same consonant sound as *cup* and *kid*. Notice how the consonant sound /k/ is spelled in each word.

Practice the Words

1. Write the words that begin or end with **c**.
2. Write the words that end like *black*.
3. Write the word that ends with *ten*.
4. Write the word that rhymes with *lid*.

Sum Up What did you learn about how the consonant sound /k/ may be spelled?

More Practice

For Extra Practice, see page 193.

Write the list word that belongs in each group.

1. shoe, slipper, ____
2. dish, glass, ____
3. pet, puppy, ____
4. leg, neck, ____
5. calf, cub, ____
6. chicken, goose, ____

Write the list word for each clue.

7. hit with your foot
8. large stone
9. choose
10. below your head
11. outdoor meal
12. not well

Word Building

Listen for the **-ock** in <u>**sock**</u>. Add **-ock** to make a new word.

1. bl ____ 2. cl ____

Listen for the **-ack** in <u>**back**</u>. Add **-ack** to make a new word.

1. p ____ 2. st ____

7 Application

cup
kid
back
duck
sock
kitten

neck
kick
sick
pick
rock
picnic

Spelling Connections

Spelling and Thinking Skills

Inferences Sometimes if you know part of a word, you can guess what the whole word means. For example, by knowing what *neck* means, you may guess that a *necktie* is a tie that is worn around the neck. Write a meaning for each word below.

1. backbone ___
2. kickball ___

Spelling and Dictionary Skills

Alphabetizing The words in a dictionary are listed in alphabetical order. Look at the first letters in the group of words below. Then write the words in alphabetical order.

duck
cup
picnic
kitten

Spelling and Writing

Which kitten would you choose for a pet? Write three sentences. Use list words such as *back*, *pick*, and *neck*. Revise and proofread your sentences.

Review and Extend

Checkup

Write a list word by adding the missing letters **c, k,** or **ck**.

1. _itten	**4.** _id	**7.** pi_ni_	**10.** pi__
2. du__	**5.** _up	**8.** si__	**11.** ro__
3. ba__	**6.** so__	**9.** ne__	**12.** _i__

Bonus Words

bike
like
kite

Write the bonus words to finish the story.

I rode my __(1)__ to the park.
Ann came too. We flew our __(2)__.
I __(3)__ to go to the park.

Challenge Words Language Arts

period
capital
question
sentence
statement

Write the word to answer each question.

1. What kind of letter starts all sentences?
2. What is a sentence that tells something?
3. What is a group of words that go together?
4. What kind of sentence asks something?
5. What comes at the end of a statement?

8 Words with Two Consonants

Introduction

Focus Some consonant sounds are spelled with two letters that are the same.

Say the Words

Listen for the consonant sounds spelled **ll, ss, ff, dd, gg,** and **bb**.

1. well	7. bell
2. hill	8. tell
3. miss	9. will
4. off	10. pass
5. add	11. egg
6. guess	12. rabbit

Wild Words Notice which consonant sounds are spelled with two letters in *guess* and *rabbit*. Remember the letter **u** in *guess*.

Practice the Words

1. Write the words with a **short a** sound.
2. Write the words with a **short e** sound.
3. Write the words that rhyme with *fill*.
4. Write the word that ends like *cuff*.
5. Write the word that rhymes with *kiss*.

Sum Up What did you learn about how some consonant sounds may be spelled?

More Practice

For Extra Practice, see page 195.

Write the list word for each clue.

1. quit, end, ___
2. shirt, pants, ___
3. float, dive, ___
4. touch, taste, ___
5. teacher, children, ___
6. hike, go up, ___

Write the list word that rhymes.

7. map
8. rock
9. bell
10. rose
11. pep
12. bag

Word Building

Listen for the **cl-** in <u>**class**</u>. Add **cl-** to make a new word.

1. ___ ick
2. ___ own

Listen for the **sw-** in <u>**swim**</u>. Add **sw-** to make a new word.

1. ___ eep
2. ___ eet

9 Application

Spelling Connections

class
dress
smell
stop
swim
climb

clap
clock
drag
step
swell
clothes

Spelling and Thinking Skills

Generalizations Some words may have endings added.

climb climb**s** climb**ing** climb**ed** climb**er**

Write the list word in each word below.

1. swimmer **2.** classes **3.** claps

Spelling and Dictionary Skills

Alphabetizing When the first letter of a group of words begins with the same letter, look at the second letter. Put the words in alphabetical order using the second letter.

d**a**nce
d**i**sh
d**o**ctor
d**r**ag
d**u**ck

Put each group of words below in alphabetical order.

1. clap cry chair **2.** slow swell step

Spelling and Writing

What are the children in the picture doing? Write three sentences. Use list words such as *dress*, *clothes*, and *class*. Revise and proofread your sentences.

Review and Extend

Checkup

Write a list word by adding the missing letters.

1. cli__	4. dre__
2. __ell	5. __op
3. cla__	6. __im

7. __othes	10. __ap
8. swe__	11. __ag
9. clo__	12. __ep

Bonus Words

club
frog
from
slow

Write the bonus word that fits in each shape.

1. 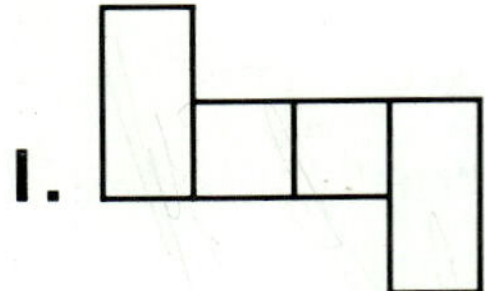

2.

3. 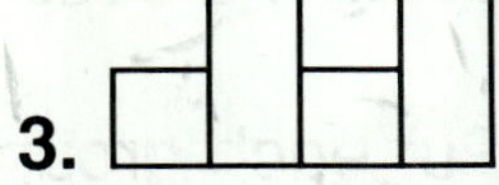

4. 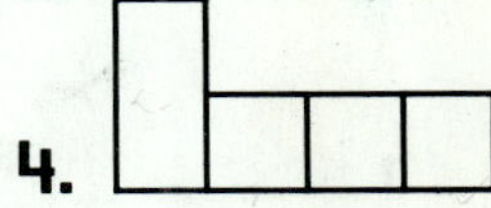

Challenge Words Health

jacket
turtleneck
scarves
gloves
shoelaces

Write the word for each definition.

1. worn on hands
2. worn over clothes
3. worn in shoes
4. worn around necks
5. sweater with a high neck

Words Ending with mp, nd, nt, sk, st

Introduction

Focus Some words end with consonants pronounced together.

lamp **bend** **tent** **mask** **test**

Say the Words

Listen for the ending sound in each word.

1. jump
2. end
3. went
4. ask
5. just
6. friend

7. stamp
8. hand
9. land
10. desk
11. must
12. different

Wild Words You may not say or hear all the letters in *friend* and *different*. Remember to write all the letters in these words.

Practice the Words

1. Write the words that end like *lamp*.
2. Write the words that end like *find*.
3. Write the words that end like *ant*.
4. Write the words that end like *mask*.
5. Write the words that end like *last*.

Sum Up What did you learn about how some ending sounds may be spelled?

For Extra Practice, see page 196.

Write the list word to finish each sentence.

1. Let's ___ mom if we can go.
2. We ___ to the circus.
3. I know the ___ of the story.
4. How far can you ___?
5. Ann is my best ___.
6. We will ___ have to wait.

Follow the clues. Write the list word.

7. am − a + ust =
8. than − t + d =
9. last − la + amp =
10. rode − ro + sk =
11. differ + enter − er =
12. plan − p + d =

Word Building

Listen for the **-st** in **just**.
Add **-st** to make a new word.

1. cru ___ 2. fir ___

Listen for the **-nd** in **end**.
Add **-nd** to make a new word.

1. po ___ 2. sta ___

10 Application

Spelling Connections

jump
end
went
ask
just
friend

stamp
hand
land
desk
must
different

Spelling and Thinking Skills

Classifying Some words are nouns. They name people, places, and things. Some words are verbs. They show action.

Add two list words to each group.

Nouns boy city car **Verbs** run hop swim

Spelling and Dictionary Skills

Alphabetizing These groups of words are alphabetized to the second letter.

art	fire
ask	fox
away	friend

Where would you add each of the following words? Finish each sentence with the correct word.

1. *Ate* comes after ___
2. *Fun* comes after ___

Spelling and Writing

Imagine that you are the rider on the horse. Write three sentences about it. Use list words such as *jump*, *hand*, and *must*. Revise and proofread your sentences.

Review and Extend

Checkup

Write a list word by adding the missing letters **mp, nd, nt, sk,** or **st**.

1. ju__
2. ju__
3. e__
4. we__
5. a__
6. frie__

7. la__
8. mu__
9. sta__
10. differe__
11. de__
12. ha__

Bonus Words

sent
tent
send
sat

Use the underlined letters to write bonus words.

1. Horses are fun to ride.
2. Some horses are trained for rodeos and horse shows.
3. Some work on cattle ranches too.
4. Horses are very useful, even today.

Challenge Words Science

starfish
tadpoles
lobster
octopus
whale

Write the word for each meaning.

1. baby frogs
2. largest living animal
3. an animal with eight arms
4. an ocean animal that has claws
5. an ocean animal with five arms

11 Words Beginning with ch, sh, th, wh

Introduction

Focus Some consonant sounds are made by two letters pronounced as one.

chair **shoe** **thing** **white**

Say the Words

Listen for the beginning consonant sounds.

1. chin	7. check
2. shall	8. shop
3. them	9. shell
4. then	10. thick
5. when	11. where
6. what	12. wear

Wild Words The words *where* and *wear* sound almost alike. Notice how each word is spelled.

Practice the Words

1. Write the words that begin like *chair* or *shoe*.
2. Write the words that begin like *they* or *why*.
3. Write the wild word that ends with **r**.

Sum Up What did you learn about how some consonant sounds at the beginning of words may be spelled?

More Practice

For Extra Practice, see page 197.

Write the list word that rhymes.

1. stem
2. pin
3. pal
4. pen
5. but
6. men

Write the list word for each clue.

7. put on clothes
8. not thin
9. a mark
10. a hard covering
11. buy
12. here or there

Word Building

Listen for the **ch-** in **chin**. Add **ch-** to make a new word.

1. ___ ill
2. ___ air

Listen for the **sh-** in **shall**. Add **sh-** to make a new word.

1. ___ are
2. ___ ore

Spelling Connections

11 Application

chin
shall
them
then
when
what

check
shop
shell
thick
where
wear

Spelling and Language Skills

Word Order in Questions The words in a question are in order and make sense.

This is a question.	This is not a question.
Who is that?	You are how?

Proofreading Write each sentence correctly. Check for capital letters, question marks, and spelling.

1. wat your name is

2. Live you do wher.

Spelling and Handwriting Skills

Write **m** and **n**. Start both letters at the middle line. The letter **m** has two hills. The letter **n** has one hill.

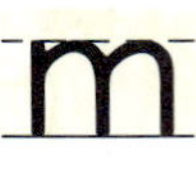

n

Then write *them*.

Spelling and Writing

Imagine the girl in the picture is a new student in your class. Write three questions you might ask her to make her feel welcome. Use list words such as *when*, *what*, and *where*. Revise and proofread your sentences.

Review and Extend

Checkup

Write a list word by adding the missing letters.

1. w__t	4. c__n
2. t__n	5. s___l
3. t__m	6. w__n

7. s__p	10. w___e
8. t___k	11. s___l
9. w__r	12. c___k

Bonus Words

the
this
that

Write the bonus word that fits in each word shape.

1.  2.  3. 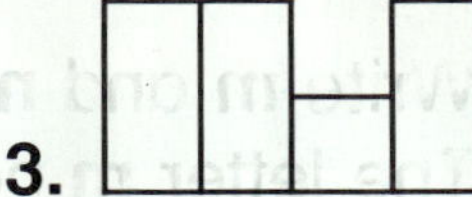

Challenge Words Reading

pirate
dragon
castle
prince
princess

Write the words to finish the story.

On the Sea of Where sailed a mean, wicked __(1)__ named Pat. Pat was looking for the last __(2)__, Poof, who lived below the sea. If Pat could capture Poof, he would become a handsome __(3)__. He would live in a __(4)__ on a high hill. He would marry a beautiful __(5)__. They would rule happily together.

12 Review

Spelling Strategy

Picturing Words Look at the letters in a word like *bill*. Look at the order of the letters. Close your eyes. Picture the order of the letters.

Activity Look at the next page. Write the words in Lesson 8 in which you see the pattern **ill**.

1. ___ 2. ___

Words with c, k, and ck Words with the consonant sound /k/ in **car**, **kite**, and **black** may be spelled with **c**, **k**, and **ck**.

7

cup **kid** **back** **duck** **sock** **kitten**

Each word below rhymes with a list word. Write the list word by adding the missing letters. Complete each word with **c**, **k**, or **ck**.

1. pup _up
2. luck du_ _
3. sack ba_ _
4. lock so_ _
5. mitten _itten
6. bid _id

neck **kick** **sick** **pick** **rock** **picnic**

Write the list words that rhyme with *tick*.

7. ___ 8. ___ 9. ___

Write a list word by adding the missing letters. Underline the letters that make the sound /k/.

10. n_ _ _ 11. _o_ _ 12. _i_ni_

Words with Two Consonants Some consonant sounds are spelled with two letters that are the same.

8

well **hill** **miss** **off** **add** **guess**

Add two letters to complete each list word.

1. o__ 2. we__ 3. a__ 4. gue__ 5. hi__ 6. mi__

bell **tell** **will** **pass** **egg** **rabbit**

Write the words below. Then circle the list words in them.

leggings rabbits telling doorbell passes willing

7. ___ 9. ___ 11. ___
8. ___ 10. ___ 12. ___

Words Beginning with cl, dr, sm, st, sw Some words begin with two consonants pronounced together.

Write the list words by adding the missing letters. Then circle the two consonants pronounced together.

9

class **smell** **swim**
dress **stop** **climb**

1. __op 4. __ell
2. __im 5. __ess
3. cla__ 6. __imb

clap **drag** **swell**
clock **step** **clothes**

7. __ep 10. __ock
8. __oth_s 11. swe__
9. dr__ 12. __ap

Words Ending with mp, nd, nt, sk, st

Some words end with two consonants that are pronounced together.

10

jump **end** **went** **ask** **just** **friend**

Write the list word that rhymes with each word.
Circle the consonants that are pronounced together.

tent **1.** ___ lump **3.** ___
bend **2.** ___ mask **4.** ___

Write the list words that rhyme with *bend*.
Underline the consonants that are pronounced together.

5. ___ **6.** ___

Write the list word that ends in **st**. **6a.** ___

stamp **hand** **land** **desk** **must** **different**

Write the list word for each clue.

7. part of the body
8. have to
9. not the same
10. used to write on
11. used to mail a letter
12. opposite of *water*

7. ___ **9.** ___ **11.** ___
8. ___ **10.** ___ **12.** ___

Words Beginning with ch, sh, th, wh Some words begin with two consonants pronounced together.

11

chin **shall** **them** **then** **when** **what**

Write the list word in which you hear the sound /sh/.
Write the list word in which you hear the sound /ch/.

1. ___ 2. ___

Complete the two sentences. Write the missing list words that begin with **wh**.

Tell us ___ you leave. Tell them ___ you saw.

3. ___ 4. ___

Write the list word by adding **th**.

5. I told _ _em I would go. 6. They were happy _ _en.

check **shop** **shell** **thick** **where** **wear**

Write the list words that rhyme.

pick bell hop

7. ___ 8. ___ 9. ___

Write the list word that begins with **ch**. 10. ___

Write the list words by adding the missing letters.

11. W____ can I go? 12. When will I w___ this?

Spelling Connections

Reading A Description of a Person

How do you describe someone? You can tell how the person looks, feels, or acts. You can use adjectives like *cheerful*, *friendly*, *tall*, or *short*.

Stormalong the Sailor was a hero of tall tales. The sentences below describe how tall he was as a boy. Read the description.

Stormalong never was a small baby. So as a boy, he got bigger and bigger. Some people say he was one of the biggest boys in America. Stormalong got so big, his head touched the sky.

from *Stormalong the Sailor* as told by
Mary Hynes-Berry

Answer the question.
What adjectives could you use to describe Stormalong's size?

Speaking and Listening

Work with a friend. Talk about ways to describe each other. You might tell each other things you like to do.

Writing A Description of a Person

Write a description of your friend. Write so that your classmates can guess who you are describing. Follow these steps.

Prewriting Think of the ideas you talked about with your friend. List the ones you want to use. Make a word bank of adjectives that describe your friend. Choose the words you can use from the spelling review list.

Writing Write your description. Choose ideas from your lists.

Revising Read the description to your friend. Make changes both of you think make the description better. Check your spelling of the review words. Use the checklists on pages 176 and 177.

Presenting Trade descriptions with another classmate. Read the new description aloud. Let the class guess who is described.

Review Words

well
guess
class
went
just
friend
them
then
when
what

13 Words Ending with ch, sh, th, ng

Introduction

Focus Some ending sounds are made by two letters pronounced as one.

such **dish** **path** **wing**

Say the Words

Listen for the ending sounds **ch, sh, th,** and **ng**.

1. much	7. inch
2. which	8. wish
3. fish	9. sing
4. bath	10. bring
5. thing	11. long
6. think	12. nothing

Wild Words The word *think* begins like *thing* but has a different ending sound. The words *no* and *thing* make up the word *nothing*.

Practice the Words

1. Write the words that end like *such*.
2. Write the words that end like *wash*.
3. Write the word that ends like *path*.
4. Write the words that end like *rang*.
5. Write the word that rhymes with *pink*.

Sum Up What did you learn about how two consonants at the end of words may be spelled?

 For Extra Practice, see page 198.

Write the correct list word to finish each sentence.

1. What do you ___?
2. How ___ did it cost?
3. What is that ___?
4. You caught a ___!
5. Tell me ___ is yours.
6. Did you take a ___?

Write the list word for each clue. The letters in the box answer the riddle written below.

7. you can do this to a song
8. not anything
9. come with something
10. want
11. part of a foot
12. not short

7. _ _ _ _
8. _ _ _ _ _ _ _
9. _ _ _ _ _
10. _ _ _ _
11. _ _ _ _
12. _ _ _ _

You can knot me, cut me, or tie me around a box. What am I? ___

Word Building

Listen for the **-sh** in **fish**. Add **-sh** to make a new word.

1. bru ___ 2. cra ___

Listen for the **-th** in **bath**. Add **-th** to make a new word.

1. mo ___ 2. mou ___

13 Application

much
which
fish
bath
thing
think

inch
wish
sing
bring
long
nothing

Spelling Connections

Spelling and Language Skills

Capitalization Special names for people and animals are called **proper nouns**. Proper nouns begin with capital letters.

Mark Jones   Ann B. Smith   Fluffy

Proofreading Read the sentences. Check for capital letters and correct spelling. Write the names and words correctly.

1. susan caught a fich today.
2. Her dog spot got nothin.

Spelling and Handwriting Skills

Write **r** and **n**. They start the same way. Write *bring*.

r n

bring

Spelling and Writing

Write three sentences about a pet you'd like to have. Use words such as *which*, *long*, and *much*. Revise and proofread your sentences.

Review and Extend

Checkup

Write a list word by adding the missing letters.

1. __ink
2. __i__
3. _i__
4. _a__
5. _u__
6. __ing
7. _o__
8. i___
9. nothi__
10. s___
11. wi__
12. _r___

Bonus Words

Change the underlined letter to **th**, **sh**, or **ch** to make a bonus word.

1. lip
2. win
3. mop

with
chop
ship

Challenge Words Mathematics

Write the word to answer each question.

1. Where is the tennis player?
2. Where is the football player?
3. Where is the basketball player?
4. Where is the fisherman?
5. Where is the baseball player?

first
second
third
fourth
fifth

14 Words with Vowel-Consonant-e

Introduction

Focus Many words with a long vowel sound are spelled with **vowel-consonant-e**.

save **nine** **pole**

Say the Words

Listen for the long vowel sounds.

1. make	7. made
2. take	8. gave
3. time	9. white
4. five	10. whole
5. home	11. those
6. please	12. surprise

Wild Words Be careful when you say and write the words *please* and *surprise*. Remember that the consonant sound /z/ is spelled **s**.

Practice the Words

1. Write the words with the **long a** sound.
2. Write the words with the **long i** sound.
3. Write the word with the **long e** sound.
4. Write the words with the **long o** sound.

Sum Up What did you learn about how long vowel sounds may be spelled?

More Practice

For Extra Practice, see page 199.

Write the words to finish the story.

What __(1)__ is it, __(2)__ ? I must be __(3)__ by half past __(4)__ . I will __(5)__ the bus. If I run, I will just __(6)__ it.

Write the word for each clue. The letters in the box answer the riddle written below.

7. color
8. this, that, these, ___
9. done
10. all
11. handed over
12. something not expected

7. ▢ _ _ _ _
8. _ ▢ _ _ _
9. _ ▢ _ _
10. _ _ _ ▢ _
11. _ _ ▢ _
12. _ _ _ _ _ _ _ ▢ _

We are large animals who live in the sea, but we are not fish. What are we? ___

Word Building

Listen for the **-ake** in **make**. Add **-ake** to make a new word.

1.  ___
2.  ___

Listen for the **-ive** in **five**. Add **-ive** to make a new word.

1. 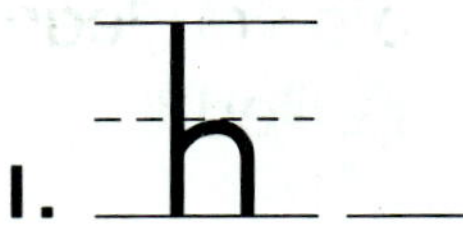 ___
2.  ___

14 Application

make
take
time
five
home
please

made
gave
white
whole
those
surprise

Spelling Connections

Spelling and Thinking Skills

Inferences The underlined word makes no sense.

I am very sleepy.
I will go to yog.

Does *yog* mean "bed," "book," or "balloon"? The clues are *sleepy* and *go*. When you are sleepy, you go to *bed*. Write a list word for each underlined word.

1. What slux is it? It is five o'clock.
2. I was very hungry. I ate the nup thing.

Spelling and Dictionary Skills

Guide Words The guide words in a dictionary tell the first word and the last word on the page.

fan

hat

fan **1.** an instrument or appliance that stirs the air in order to cool it. **2.** stir the air. **3.** use as a fan: *He fanned himself with his hat.* **fans; fanned, fan ning.**

1. What are the guide words on this page?
2. What list words would go on this page?

Spelling and Writing

Write several sentences telling about a party. Use list words such as *five*, *gave*, and *surprise*. Revise and proofread your sentences.

Review and Extend

Checkup

Write a list word by adding the missing letters.

1. pl_ _s_	4. h_m_	7. th_s_	10. m_d_
2. m_k_	5. t_k_	8. wh_t_	11. surpr_s_
3. t_m_	6. f_v_	9. g_v_	12. wh_l_

Bonus Words

nine
hope
rode
nose

Change one letter to make a bonus word.

1. note
2. nice
3. rose
4. home

Challenge Words Science

hour
month
o'clock
minutes
calendar

Write the words to finish the invitation.

Dear Aunt Jane,

We are having a party for Beth. Mark your (1) for the (2) of June. The party will begin at 4 (3) on the 5th. Please come one (4) early to help us. It will take about fifty (5) to get ready. We hope you can come.

Love,

Tom

15 Words with Long a

Introduction

Focus These words have the **long a** sound in **pail** and **day**.

- **Long a** may be spelled **ai** and **ay**.

Say the Words

Listen for the **long a** sound.

1. rain
2. mail
3. way
4. may
5. play
6. they
7. wait
8. train
9. plain
10. paint
11. stay
12. eight

Wild Words Be careful when you say and write the words *they* and *eight*. **Long a** is spelled **ey** in *they* and **eigh** in *eight*.

Practice the Words

1. Write the words with **long a** spelled **ai**. Circle the **ai**.
2. Write the words with **long a** spelled **ay**. Underline the **ay**.
3. Write the words with **long a** not spelled **ai** or **ay**.

Sum Up What did you learn about how **long a** may be spelled?

More Practice

For Extra Practice, see page 200.

Follow the clues. Write the list word.

1. sway − s =
2. tray − tr + m =
3. replay − re =
4. train − t =
5. m + sail − s =
6. the + my − m =

Complete each phrase with a list word.

1. ___ inches
2. ___ calm
3. the ___ station
4. a ___ store
5. a very short ___
6. a ___ cracker

Word Building

Listen for the **-ain** in rain. Add **-ain** to make a new word.

1. m ___
2. gr ___

Listen for the **-ay** in way. Add **-ay** to make a new word.

1. cl ___
2. gr ___

15 Application

Spelling Connections

rain
mail
way
may
play
they

wait
train
plain
paint
stay
eight

Spelling and Language Skills

Capitalization Special names for places are called **proper nouns**. Proper nouns begin with capital letters.

Miami, Florida   Elm School   Coal City Library

Proofreading Read the sentences. Check for capital letters and spelling. Write the sentences.

1. We may see a plai in New york.
2. Uncle joe will meet our train.

Spelling and Handwriting Skills

Write the letters **p** and **g**. Both letters go below the bottom line. Write *paint* and *eight*.

Spelling and Writing

Write three sentences about a trip you'd like to take. Use list words such as *train*, *play*, and *stay*. Revise and proofread your sentences.

Review and Extend

Checkup

Write a list word by adding the missing letter or letters.

1. th__	4. m_y
2. pl__	5. m__l
3. r__n	6. w_y

7. ___t	10. tr__n
8. st_y	11. w__t
9. pl__n	12. p__nt

Bonus Words

Write the bonus word for each clue.

1. talk, speak, ___
2. Joan A. Jones
3. Monday or Tuesday
4. arrived

name
came
say
day

Challenge Words Social Studies

Write the word to finish each sentence.

1. My uncle needed ___ to get to our house.
2. He looked at a ___ to help him find us.
3. Uncle Jim is buying a house on our ___.
4. The park in our ___ is two streets away.
5. We go to the ___ center for parties.

block
map
community
directions
neighborhood

16 Words with Long e

Introduction

Focus These words have the **long e** sound in **bee**, **sea**, and **he**.

- **Long e** may be spelled **ee**, **ea**, and **e**.

Say the Words

Listen for the **long e** sound.

1. keep
2. feel
3. read
4. eat
5. she
6. three

7. teeth
8. green
9. team
10. mean
11. each
12. between

Wild Words The words *three* and *between* have the **long e** sound. The first **e** in *between* is not a **long e** sound. It is a **short i** sound spelled **e**.

Practice the Words

1. Write the words with **long e** spelled **ee**.
2. Write the words with **long e** spelled **ea**.
3. Write the word with **long e** spelled **e**.

Sum Up What did you learn about how **long e** may be spelled?

For Extra Practice, see page 201.

Write the list word that fits in each word shape.

1. 

3. 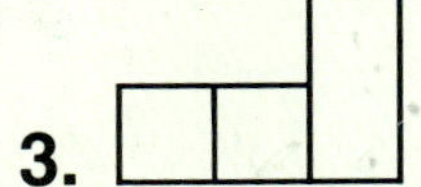

5. 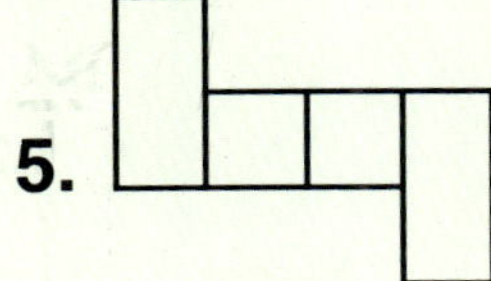

2. 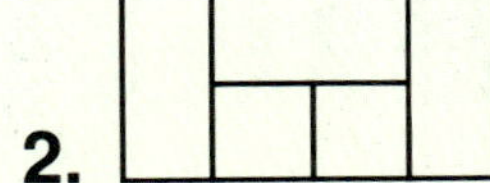

4. 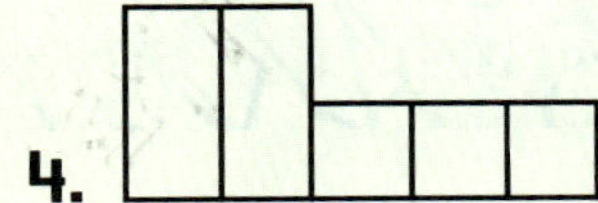

6. 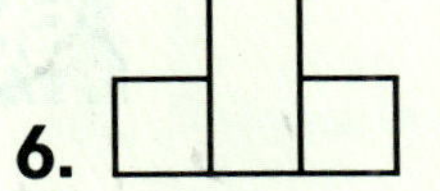

Write the list word for each clue.

7. in the middle of
8. used for chewing
9. not nice
10. every or all
11. yellow mixed with blue
12. people working together

Word Building

Listen for the **-eel** in **feel**. Add **-eel** to make a new word.

1. 

2. 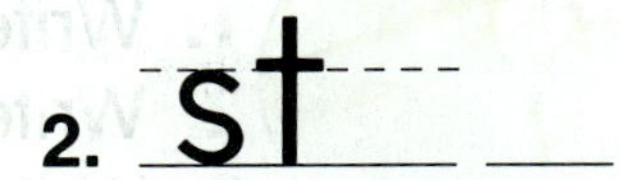

Listen for the **-eep** in **keep**. Add **-eep** to make a new word.

1. 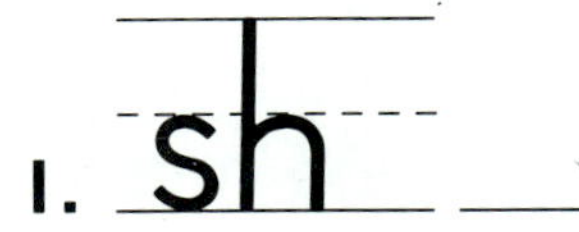

2. sw ___

Spelling Connections

keep
feel
read
eat
she
three

teeth
green
team
mean
each
between

Spelling and Thinking Skills

Generalizations How are these words the same? How are they different?

seen seed seek seem seep sees

All the words begin the same way. The final consonant is different.

Make a new word by changing the final consonant. Use the consonants **d**, **l**, and **n**.

1. feet **2.** real **3.** greet

Spelling and Dictionary Skills

Parts of an Entry A dictionary entry tells you many things about an entry word.

definitions

entry word — **feel** **1.** touch: *Feel the smooth stone.* **2.** be; have in the mind: *She feels sad. I have felt sad too.* **feels, felt, feel ing.**

special forms

1. What is the entry word shown above?
2. How many definitions are there?
3. How many special forms does the entry show?

Spelling and Writing

Write three sentences about a book you have read. Use list words such as *green*, *teeth*, and *mean*. Revise and proofread your sentences.

Review and Extend

Checkup

Write a list word by adding the missing letters **ee**, **ea**, or **e**.

1. thr__	4. __t	7. __ch	10. t__m
2. f__l	5. sh_	8. t__th	11. betw__n
3. r__d	6. k__p	9. m__n	12. gr__n

Bonus Words

need
he
me
we

Write the bonus word for each clue.

1. myself
2. Bob
3. Jane and I
4. must have

Challenge Words Mathematics

count
addition
sum
numeral
million

Write the word for each meaning.

1. total
2. say numbers one by one
3. very large number
4. putting two groups together
5. symbol for a number

17 Words with Long i

Introduction

Focus These words have the **long i** sound in **kind**, **sky**, and **might**.

- **Long i** may be spelled **i**, **y**, and **igh**.

Say the Words

Listen for the **long i** sound.

1. find	7. mind
2. kind	8. why
3. cry	9. high
4. try	10. light
5. right	11. night
6. eyes	12. behind

Wild Words The words *eyes* and *behind* have the **long i** sound. **Long i** is spelled **ey** in *eyes* and **i** in *behind*.

Practice the Words

1. Write the words that end like *sand*.
2. Write the words that rhyme with *I*.
3. Write the words that rhyme with *kite*.
4. Write the word that rhymes with *size*.

Sum Up What did you learn about how **long i** may be spelled?

For Extra Practice, see page 202.

Follow the clues. Write the list word.

1. kite − te + nd =
2. be + yes − b =
3. fine − e + d =
4. trap − ap + y =
5. rip − p + ght =
6. car − a + y =

Write the list word for each clue.

7. at the back of
8. listen
9. lamp
10. far above
11. evening
12. when, where, ___

Word Building

Listen for the **-ind** in **kind**. Add **-ind** to make a new word.

1. gr ___
2. bl ___

Listen for the **-y** in **cry**. Add **-y** to make a new word.

1. fr ___
2. sh ___

17 Application

Spelling Connections

find
kind
cry
try
right
eyes

mind
why
high
light
night
behind

Spelling and Language Skills

Capitalization Begin the names of days with a capital letter.

Sunday Monday Tuesday Wednesday

Thursday Friday Saturday

Proofreading Read the sentences. Check for capital letters and spelling. Write the sentences correctly.

1. On friday we went to fin a pumpkin.
2. On saturday nite we carved it.

Spelling and Handwriting Skills

Write **w** and **y**. Start both letters at the middle line. The tail of the letter **y** goes below the bottom line. Then write *why*.

w y

why

Spelling and Writing

Write three sentences about a game you might play. Use list words such as *find*, *try*, and *eyes*. Revise and proofread your sentences.

Review and Extend

Checkup

Write a list word by adding the missing letters **i**, **y**, or **igh**.

1. e_es	**4.** tr_
2. k_nd	**5.** r___t
3. cr_	**6.** f_nd

7. wh_	**10.** l___t
8. beh_nd	**11.** m_nd
9. h___	**12.** n___t

Bonus Words

Write the bonus words to finish the story.

Yesterday __(1)__ friend and __(2)__ went to the park. We went on a pony __(3)__. Mike and I had a __(4)__ time.

I
my
fine
ride

Challenge Words Social Studies

Write the word for each meaning.

1. mother or father

2. father's sister

3. mother's father

4. mother's child

5. child of uncle

grandfather
cousin
aunt
daughter
parent

18 Review

Spelling Strategy

Listening to Words Always *listen* to the sounds in a word. Say the word out loud. Think about the letter or letters that make each sound.

Activity In which words in Lesson 13 below do you hear the sound /sh/?

1. ___ **2.** ___

Words Ending with ch, sh, th, ng Some words end with two consonants that are pronounced together.

13

much	**which**	**fish**	**bath**	**thing**	**think**

Write the list words that begin or end with **th**.

1. ___ **2.** ___ **3.** ___

Write the list words by adding the missing letters. Circle the end consonants that are pronounced together.

4. mu__ **5.** w__ch **6.** __sh

inch	**wish**	**sing**	**bring**	**long**	**nothing**

Write the list words by adding the missing letters. Underline the end consonants that are pronounced together.

7. no__ing **9.** lo__ **11.** b__ng
8. __ch **10.** wi__ **12.** s__g

Words with Vowel-Consonant-e Many words with a long vowel sound are spelled with **vowel-consonant-e**.

14

make **take** **time** **five** **home** **please**

Make a list word from each clue. Then underline the **vowel-consonant-e**.

mat + ke − t

1. ___

fir − r + ve

2. ___

tall + ke − ll

3. ___

ho + men − n

4. ___

tin + me − n

5. ___

Which list word has a consonant sound /z/? **6.** ___

made **gave** **white** **whole** **those** **surprise**

First, write the list words that have the **long a** sound.
Next, write the list words that have the **long o** sound.
Last, write the list words that have the **long i** sound.
Then underline the **vowel-consonant-e** that makes the long vowel sound.

7. ___
8. ___
9. ___
10. ___
11. ___
12. ___

Words with Long a The words **pail** and **day** have the **long a** sound. **Long a** may be spelled **ai** and **ay**.

15

rain **mail** **way** **may** **play** **they**

Write the list words that end in **ay**. Circle the letters that make the **long a** sound.

1. ___ 2. ___ 3. ___

Write the list words by adding the missing letters that make the **long a** sound.

4. r__n 5. m__l 6. th__

wait **train** **plain** **paint** **stay** **eight**

Write the list words by adding the missing letters. Circle the letters that make the **long a** sound.

7. w__t
8. _lai_
9. eigh_
10. tr__n
11. p___t
12. st__

Words with Long e The words **bee**, **sea**, and **he** have the **long e** sound spelled **ee**, **ea**, and **e**.

Write the list words by adding the missing letters in each word. Circle the letter or letters that make the **long e** sound.

16

keep **read** **she**
feel **eat** **three**

1. k__p
2. __ree
3. r__d
4. s__
5. f__l
6. __t

teeth **team** **each**
green **mean** **between**

7. gr__n
8. ea__
9. be__een
10. t__th
11. m__n
12. t__m

Speaking and Listening

Work with a partner. Describe something or some place special to you. It might be something you made or a place where you play. Let your partner ask questions. Use your answers in your description.

Writing A Description of a Special Place or Thing

Write your description and read it to your classmates. Follow these steps.

Prewriting List things you want to say and things your partner wanted to know. Make a word bank of adjectives and adverbs you might use. Add some spelling words.

Writing Write your description. Choose ideas from your lists.

Revising Read your description to a partner. Ask your partner to draw the place or thing you described. Revise your description if the picture is not correct. Check your spelling of the review words. Use the checklists on pages 176 and 177.

Presenting Work in small groups. Read your description aloud. You may want to show your partner's picture.

Review Words

much
which
thing
think
make
home
play
keep
feel
right

19 Words with Long o

Introduction

Focus These words have the **long o** sound in **no**, **coat**, and **slow**.

- **Long o** may be spelled **o**, **oa**, and **ow**.

Say the Words

Listen for the **long o** sound.

1.	most	7.	hold
2.	told	8.	old
3.	goat	9.	both
4.	boat	10.	grow
5.	show	11.	own
6.	know	12.	only

Wild Words The words *know* and *only* have the **long o** sound. Notice that the sound /n/ in *know* is spelled **kn**.

Practice the Words

1. Write the words with **long o** spelled **o**.
2. Write the words with **long o** spelled **oa**.
3. Write the words with **long o** spelled **ow**.

Sum Up What did you learn about how **long o** may be spelled?

 For Extra Practice, see page 203.

Write the list words that have the same meaning as the underlined words.

1. Who said that to you?
2. I ate nearly all of my lunch.
3. Mark made a small ship.
4. We're going to a play.
5. I understand how you feel.
6. We saw a kid at the farm.

Write the list words to finish the crossword puzzle.

ACROSS
1. get bigger
3. by itself
5. grab onto

DOWN
2. have
3. not young
4. two

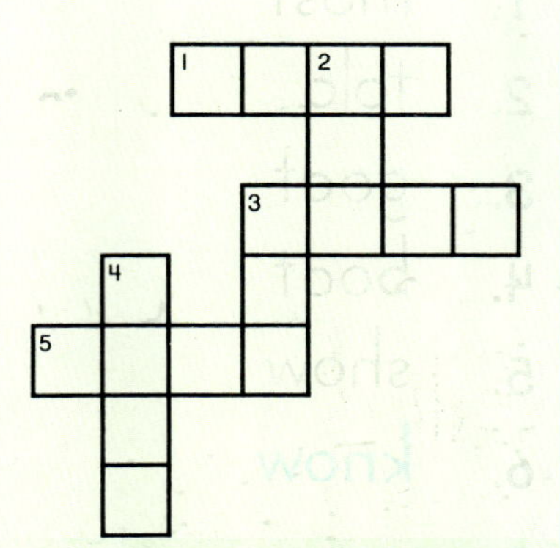

Word Building

Listen for the **-old** in **told**. Add **-old** to make a new word.

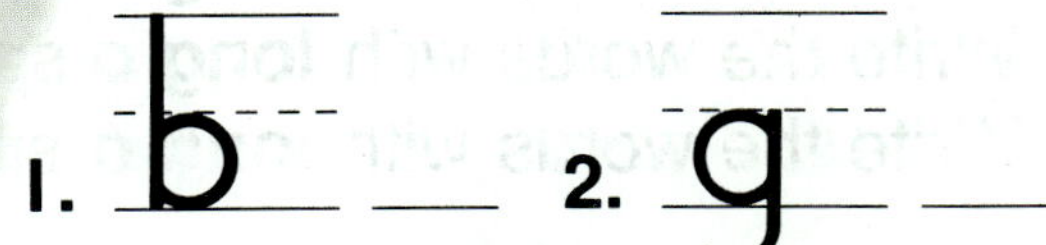

Listen for the **-ow** in **show**. Add **-ow** to make a new word.

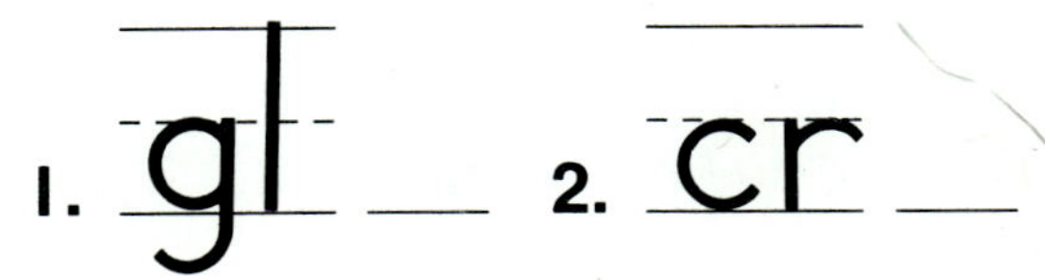

19 Application

most
told
goat
boat
show
know

hold
old
both
grow
own
only

Spelling Connections

Spelling and Thinking Skills

Classifying A new word is often made by adding a letter or letters to the beginning or end of the word.

new newest kind unkind

Look at the words *retold*, *showed*, and *owner*. Decide if letters were added to the beginning or to the end of a list word. Then complete the chart.

Beginning	Base Word	Ending
	new	est
un	kind	

Spelling and Dictionary Skills

Word Meanings Many words have more than one meaning. A dictionary entry shows the different meanings of a word.

show 1. bring or put in sight. **2.** make clear to. **3.** a play, movie, or TV program.

Write the number of the meaning for each sentence.

1. I saw a funny show.
2. Miss Lee will show us how it works.
3. Did Mike show you his new bike?

Spelling and Writing

Write three sentences about a fisherman's job. Use list words such as *boat*, *hold*, and *own*. Revise and proofread your sentences.

Review and Extend

Checkup

Write a list word by adding the missing letters **o, oa,** or **ow**.

1. kn__	**4.** m_st	**7.** _nly	**10.** _ld
2. b__t	**5.** g__t	**8.** h_ld	**11.** gr__
3. t_ld	**6.** sh__	**9.** __n	**12.** b_th

Bonus Words

Write the bonus word for each clue.

no
so
go
rode

1. very

2. move

3. not yes

4. carried along

Challenge Words Vocabulary

Write the word for each meaning.

flagpole
homework
scarecrow
toothbrush
daytime

1. lessons to do at home

2. opposite of *nighttime*

3. a flag flies from it

4. used to keep teeth clean

5. used to scare birds away

20 Vowel Sound in moon

Introduction

Focus These words have the vowel sound in **moon**.

- The vowel sound /ü/ as in **moon** may be spelled **oo** and **ew**.

Say the Words

Listen for the sound /ü/ in the list words.

1.	food	7.	cool
2.	soon	8.	moon
3.	room	9.	zoo
4.	tool	10.	flew
5.	new	11.	chew
6.	who	12.	knew

Wild Words The words *who* and *knew* have the vowel sound /ü/. Be sure to begin *who* with the letter **w**. The sound /n/ in *knew* is spelled **kn**.

Practice the Words

1. Write the words with the sound /ü/ spelled **oo**.
2. Write the words with the sound /ü/ spelled **ew**.
3. Write the word with the sound /ü/ spelled **o**.

Sum Up What did you learn about how the vowel sound /ü/ may be spelled?

 For Extra Practice, see page 204.

Write the list word for each clue.

1. which person
2. part of a house
3. helps do work
4. unused
5. before long
6. things to eat

Follow the clues. Write the list word.

7. It begins like *knot*.
   It ends like *blew*.
8. It begins like *comet*.
   It ends like *fool*.
9. It begins like *chick*.
   It ends like *stew*.
10. It begins like *mop*.
    It ends like *balloon*.
11. It begins like *zipper*.
    It ends like *coo*.
12. It begins like *flower*.
    It ends like *new*.

Word Building

Listen for the **-ew** in **new**. Add **-ew** to make a new word.

1. gr____ 2. st____

Listen for the **-oon** in **soon**. Add **-oon** to make a new word.

1. sp____ 2. cart____

20 Application

food
soon
room
tool
new
who

cool
moon
zoo
flew
chew
knew

Spelling Connections

Spelling and Language Skills

Capitalization Begin the names of months with a capital letter.

January	February	March	April
May	June	July	August
September	October	November	December

Proofreading Read the sentences. Check for capital letters and spelling. Then write the sentences correctly.

1. hoo has a birthday in july?
2. I knu Joe had one in june.

Spelling and Handwriting Skills

Write the letters **s** and **z**. Start the letter **s** just below the middle line. The letter **z** should touch the middle line. Then write *soon* and *zoo*.

s z

soon zoo

Spelling and Writing

Write three sentences about being in the woods. Use list words such as *moon*, *cool*, and *flew*. Revise and proofread your sentences.

Review and Extend

Checkup

Write a list word by adding the missing letters **o**, **oo**, or **ew**.

1. wh_
2. t__l
3. r__m
4. n__
5. f__d
6. s__n
7. kn__
8. ch__
9. c__l
10. fl__
11. z__
12. m__n

Bonus Words

do
to
you

Write the bonus word to finish each sentence.

1. I want ___ visit the zoo.
2. Do ___ want to go too?
3. What does Mom want to ___?

Challenge Words Mathematics

pennies
nickel
quarter
silver
coins

Write the word to answer each question.

1. What is another word for five cents?
2. What are nickels, pennies, and dimes called?
3. What do you need ten of to equal one dime?
4. What metal is part of some money?
5. What is another name for twenty-five cents?

21 Adding -s and -es

Introduction

Focus The endings **-s** and **-es** can give a word the added meaning "more than one."

- Add **-s** to most words.
- Add **-es** to words that end in **ch**, **sh**, and **x**.

Say the Words

Listen for the endings.

1.	boys	7.	swings
2.	lunches	8.	inches
3.	branches	9.	dishes
4.	wishes	10.	bushes
5.	foxes	11.	boxes
6.	people	12.	children

Wild Words The words *people* and *children* both already have the meaning "more than one." Notice that these words do not end with **-s** or **-es**.

Practice the Words

1. Write the words that have **-s** added.
2. Write the words that have **-es** added.
3. Write the wild words on your list.

Sum Up How can you give many words the added meaning of "more than one"?

More Practice

For Extra Practice, see page 205.

Write the list words to finish the crossword puzzle.

ACROSS
1. persons
4. parts of trees
5. wants

DOWN
2. meals at noon
3. small, sly animals
4. male children

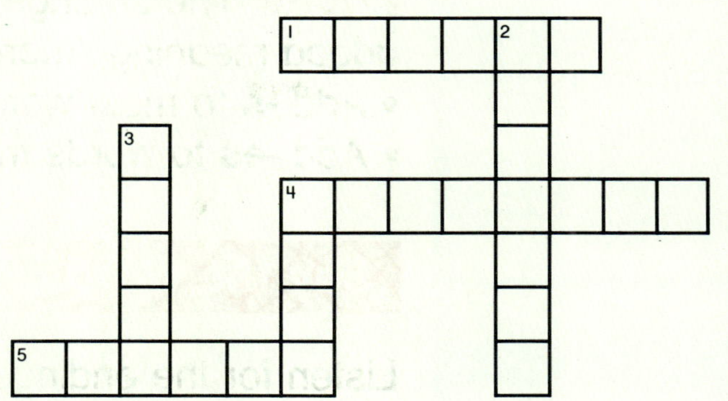

Write the list word for each clue.

1. a child + a child =
2. a swing + a swing =
3. a dish + a dish =
4. a box + a box =
5. an inch + an inch =
6. a bush + a bush =

Word Study

Make each word mean "more than one" by adding **-s** or **-es**.

1. boat
2. stamp
3. watch
4. ax

21 Application

Spelling Connections

boys
lunches
branches
wishes
foxes
people

swings
inches
dishes
bushes
boxes
children

Spelling and Thinking Skills

Classifying How are cars, buses, and trains alike? They are all forms of transportation. Look at each group of words below. Write the list word that tells how they are alike.

1.	2.	3.
men	James	plates
women	Thomas	platters
children	Robert	bowls

Spelling and Dictionary Skills

Special Forms Many words have special forms. If you want to know how to spell a special form of a word, you can look up the base word in the dictionary.

branch a part of a tree that grows out from the trunk. **branch es.**

One special form of *branch* is *branches*.

Write the entry word for each special form below.

1. lunches **2.** boys **3.** children

Spelling and Writing

Write three sentences about a playground. Use list words such as *people*, *swings*, and *children*. Revise and proofread your sentences.

Review and Extend

Checkup

Write a list word by adding the missing letters.

1. _eo__e
2. _ish__
3. _unch__
4. _o__
5. _o___
6. branch__

7. inch__
8. bush__
9. bo___
10. sw_ng_
11. dish__
12. ch_ldr_n

Bonus Words

pigs
pins
lips

Write the bonus word that fits in each word shape.

1. 2. 3.

Challenge Words Physical Education

softball
diamond
coach
field
track

Write the words to finish the puzzle.

DOWN
1. shape
3. where races are run

ACROSS
2. teacher of games
4. game played with bat and ball
5. where games are played

22 Adding -ing and -ed

Introduction

Focus The endings **-ing** and **-ed** are added to many words.

- If a word ends in **e**, drop the **e** and add **-ing** or **-ed**.

Say the Words

Listen for the endings.

1. liking
2. liked
3. smiling
4. smiled
5. making
6. hiding
7. racing
8. raced
9. using
10. used
11. catching
12. caught

Wild Words The words *catching* and *caught* are both formed from the base word *catch*. Notice that *caught* does not end in **-ed**.

Practice the Words

1. Write the words with the **-ing** ending.
2. Write the words with the **-ed** ending.
3. Write the wild word that does not end in **-ing** or **-ed**.

Sum Up What did you learn about how words ending in **-ing** and **-ed** may be spelled?

More Practice

For Extra Practice, see page 206.

Write the list word that fits in each word shape.

1. 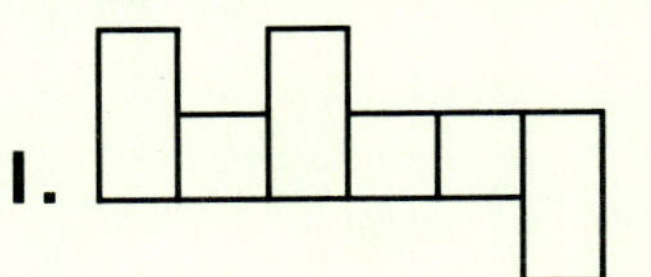

3. 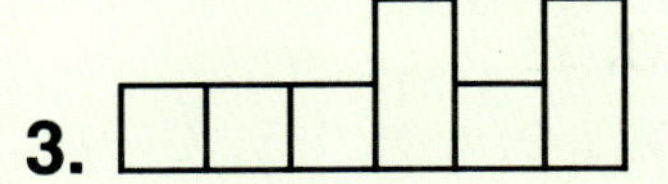

5. 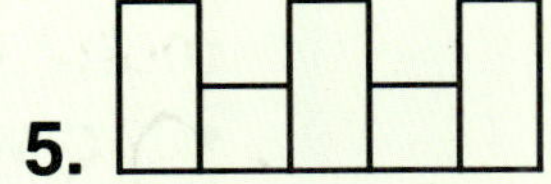

2. 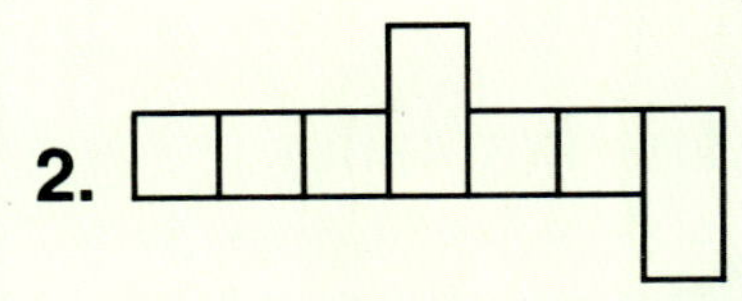

4. 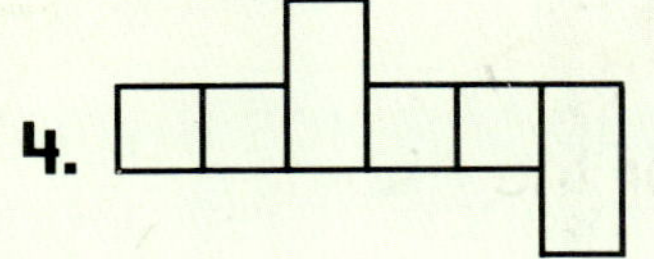

6.

Write the list words for these base words.

7.– 8. use ___ ___
9.–10. race ___ ___
11.–12. catch ___ ___

Word Study

Add **-ing** and **-ed** to each word to make two new words. Remember to drop the final **e** of a base word ending in **e**.

1.–2. wash ___ ___
3.–4. bake ___ ___

22 Application

liking
liked
smiling
smiled
making
hiding

racing
raced
using
used
catching
caught

Spelling Connections

Spelling and Thinking Skills

Generalizations Look at each group of words. How are they the same? How are they different?

blowing	flowing	glowing	slowing
keeping	beeping	peeping	weeping

Each group of words rhymes. The first letter is different in each group. Change the first letter in each word below to make a rhyming list word.

1. hiked **2.** matching **3.** taught

Spelling and Dictionary Skills

Special Forms You can use your dictionary to find the **special forms** of a word.

> **ride 1.** sit on something and make it go: *Some people ride camels.* **2.** a trip on an animal or a vehicle: *We took a ride on our bikes.* **rode, rid den, rid ing; rides** — special forms

Look up *make* in your Spelling Dictionary. Write the special forms of *make*.

Spelling and Writing

Write three sentences about playing hide-and-seek. Use list words such as *hiding*, *caught*, and *raced*. Revise and proofread your sentences.

Review and Extend

Checkup

Write a list word by adding the missing letters.

1. hid___	4. l_k__
2. smil___	5. smil__
3. lik___	6. mak___

7. us___	10. _s__
8. rac___	11. c__ght
9. catchi__	12. r_c__

Bonus Words

seemed
creeping
sleeping
riding

Write the bonus word to finish each sentence.

1. The bug is ___ slowly.
2. Mary ___ unhappy.
3. Bob is ___ his bike.
4. The baby is ___.

Challenge Words Science

helicopter
astronaut
orbit
force
motion

Write the word to finish each sentence.

1. The ___ of the rockets sent the spaceship up.
2. The spaceship went into ___ around the earth.
3. The ___ had experiments to perform.
4. She watched weightless bees in ___.
5. When she lands, a ___ will pick her up.

23 Adding -ing and -ed

Introduction

Focus The endings **-ing** and **-ed** are added to many words.

- Some words end with one vowel followed by one consonant, as **hop** and **bat** do. With words like these, double the final consonant before adding **-ing** or **-ed**.

Say the Words

Listen for the endings.

1. hopping
2. hopped
3. batting
4. batted
5. planning
6. planned
7. napping
8. napped
9. sledding
10. sledded
11. beginning
12. began

Wild Words The words *beginning* and *began* are formed from the base word *begin*.

Practice the Words

1. Write the words with the **-ed** ending.
2. Write the words with the **-ing** ending.
3. Write the word that does not end in **-ing** or **-ed**.

Sum Up What did you learn about how words ending in **-ing** and **-ed** may be spelled?

More Practice

For Extra Practice, see page 207.

Write the list word that fits with each group.

1. jumping, skipping,
2. caught, threw,
3. thinking, deciding,
4. thought, decided,
5. jumped, skipped,
6. catching, throwing,

What list word has the same meaning as the underlined word? Write the word.

7. The show is <u>starting</u> now.
8. It <u>started</u> earlier yesterday.
9. The baby is <u>resting</u> now.
10. She <u>rested</u> this morning too.
11. Ted is <u>coasting</u> down a hill.
12. May <u>coasted</u> down before him.

Word Study

Add **-ing** and **-ed** to each word to make two new words. Double the final consonant of the base word.

1.–2. stop **3.–4.** hum

23 Application

hopping
hopped
batting
batted
planning
planned

napping
napped
sledding
sledded
beginning
began

Spelling Connections

Spelling and Language Skills

Capitalization Begin the names of holidays with a capital letter.

Valentine's Day Halloween New Year's Day

Proofreading Write each sentence correctly. Check for capital letters and spelling.

1. We planed a halloween party.
2. We went sleding on new year's day.

Spelling and Handwriting Skills

Be sure to form the letter **d** carefully. If your letter is not clear, it might look like **cl**.

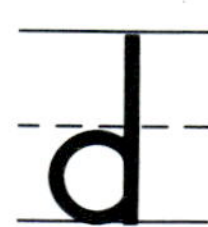

Write the word *sledding*.

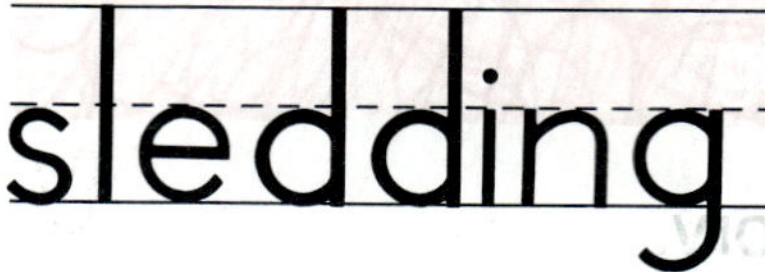

Spelling and Writing

Write three sentences about playing in the first snowfall with friends. Use words such as *planning*, *sledding*, and *sledded*. Revise and proofread your sentences.

Review and Extend

Checkup

Write a list word by adding the missing letters.

1. plan___	4. ba__ing
2. ho__ing	5. hop___
3. bat___	6. pla__ing

7. sled___	10. sle__ing
8. begi__ing	11. na__ing
9. nap___	12. be___

Bonus Words

Write the bonus word for each base word below.

getting
letting
running
cutting

1. cut
2. let
3. get
4. run

Challenge Words Reading

Write the words to finish the story.

holiday
celebration
parade
costume
mask

Oh, boy! Tomorrow is October 31st. I can wear my Halloween _(1)_. I have a scary _(2)_ to put on my face. We have a big _(3)_ at school. All the children line up and _(4)_ around the school. This is my favorite _(5)_!

24 Review

Spelling Strategy

Taking Tests In some tests you must choose a word to fill a blank in a sentence. Read the sentence and the words. Look at the letters and listen to their sounds. Choose the correct word.

Activity Read each sentence. Choose the word that fits in the blank.

We ___ the secret.
a. toll **b.** told

Two ___ played.
a. boyes **b.** boys

Words with Long o Words with the **long o** sound in **no, coat,** and **slow** may be spelled **o, oa,** and **ow.**

Study the words. Cover them. Write the words you can remember. Then write the rest of the words.

19

most **told** **goat** **boat** **show** **know**

1. ___
2. ___
3. ___
4. ___
5. ___
6. ___

hold **old** **both** **grow** **own** **only**

7. ___
8. ___
9. ___
10. ___
11. ___
12. ___

Vowel Sound in moon The vowel sound in m<u>oo</u>n may be spelled **oo** and **ew.**

Write a list word by adding the missing letter or letters.

20

food	room	new
soon	tool	who

1. s__n
2. n__
3. r__m
4. wh_
5. f__d
6. t__l

cool	zoo	chew
moon	flew	knew

7. m__n
8. c__l
9. kn__
10. fl__
11. z__
12. ch__

Adding -s and -es Add **-s** to most words to give the meaning "more than one." Add **-es** to words that end in **ch, sh,** and **x.**

Write the words. Circle the **-s** and **-es** endings. Underline any word that does not end in **-s** or **-es.**

21

boys	lunches	branches	wishes	foxes	people

1. ___
2. ___
3. ___
4. ___
5. ___
6. ___

swings	inches	dishes	bushes	boxes	children

7. ___
8. ___
9. ___
10. ___
11. ___
12. ___

Adding -ing and -ed If a word ends in **e,** drop the **e** before adding **-ing** or **ed.**

22

liking **liked** **smiling** **smiled** **making** **hiding**

Write the words that end in **-ed.** Then write the words that end in **-ing.** Circle the endings.

1. ___ 3. ___ 5. ___
2. ___ 4. ___ 6. ___

Write the words that go with these meanings.

covering up putting together

6a. ___ 6b. ___

racing **raced** **using** **used** **catching** **caught**

Decide what letters are missing. Then write the words.

u_i__ _a_i__ u_e_

7. ___ 8. ___ 9. ___

Write the words that mean the opposite of these words.

dropping **10.** ___ dropped **11.** ___

Write the word that rhymes with *chased.* **12.** ___

Adding -ing and -ed Double the final consonant before adding **-ing** or **-ed** to a word that ends with one vowel followed by a consonant.

23

hopping **hopped** **batting** **batted** **planning** **planned**

Write the word that rhymes with each word.

chatting	tanning	stopping
1. ___	**2.** ___	**3.** ___

Complete each sentence with a list word.

4. He ___ the party.
5. The rabbit ___ away.
6. The catcher ___ last.

napping **napped** **sledding** **sledded** **beginning** **began**

Write the list word that rhymes with each word.

shedding	tapping	slapped
7. ___	**8.** ___	**9.** ___

Decide what letters are missing. Then write the list word.

beg_ _ning	_ _edded	beg_ _
10. ___	**11.** ___	**12.** ___

Spelling Connections

Reading A Friendly Letter

In this lesson, you will write a letter about a time that is special to you. Your letter will have five parts—a date, greeting, body, closing, and name.

Below is a letter Phoebe Dormouse wrote to her mother. Phoebe had grown up and found a home of her own. She wrote her mother the day she moved.

Dear Mother,

I'm in my new home and it's snug and warm. All my things are unpacked and put away very neatly. I like being grown-up.

Good night,
Phoebe

from *Dear Phoebe* by Sue Alexander

Answer the question.
Find these parts of Phoebe's letter: greeting, body, closing, and name. Tell what each part says. Which part did Phoebe leave out?

Speaking and Listening

Work with a partner. Tell about a time that was special to you. Let your partner ask questions. Use your answers in your letter.

Writing A Friendly Letter

Write a letter to a friend telling about your special time. Follow these steps.

Prewriting List the things you want to say and things your partner wanted to know. Choose spelling words that will help you.

Writing Write your letter to a friend. Put the date in the upper right-hand corner. Use all the parts of a letter that Phoebe used. Choose ideas from your lists.

Revising Exchange letters with your partner. Look for ways to make both letters better. Use the checklists on pages 176 and 177.

Presenting Write an envelope with your friend's mailing address and your return address. Add a stamp. Mail your letter.

Review Words

most
told
show
know
soon
new
who
wishes
people
liked

25 Compound Words

Introduction

Focus A **compound word** is two words that are put together to make another word.

play + ground = playground

Say the Words

Listen for the two words in each compound word.

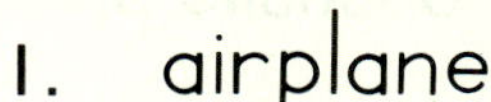

1. airplane
2. inside
3. myself
4. cannot
5. birthday
6. anything

7. sunshine
8. nobody
9. sometimes
10. something
11. into
12. everyone

Wild Words Notice that the **short e** sound in *anything* is spelled **a**. Be sure to write all the letters in *everyone*.

Practice the Words

1. Write the words from 1 to 6 in alphabetical order.
2. Write the words from 7 to 12 that begin with a vowel.
3. Write the words from 7 to 12 that begin with a consonant.

Sum Up How are compound words formed?

More Practice

For Extra Practice, see page 208.

airplane inside myself cannot birthday anything

Put two words together to make a list word.

any	not	thing	air	my	self
in	can	side	birth	day	plane

sunshine nobody sometimes something into everyone

Write the list word that means the opposite of these words.

7. no one
8. somebody
9. nothing
10. never
11. out of
12. moonlight

Word Building

Add **-way** to each word below to make a compound word.

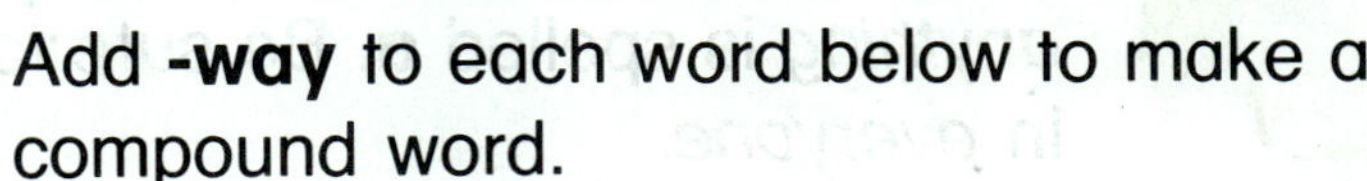

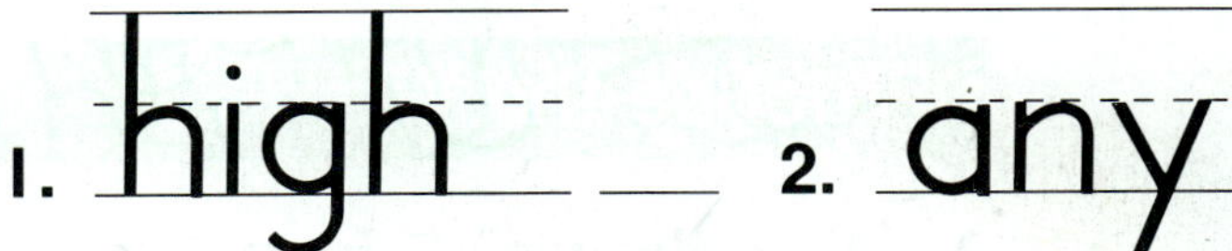

Add **black-** to the word below to make a compound word.

airplane
inside
myself
cannot
birthday
anything

sunshine
nobody
sometimes
something
into
everyone

Spelling Connections

Spelling and Thinking Skills

Generalizations When you hear one word, sometimes it makes you think of another. For example, you may think of a word with the opposite meaning. Write the list word you think of when you read each word below.

1. outside
2. can
3. somebody

Spelling and Dictionary Skills

Word Meaning Many words have more than one meaning. Look up the word *into* in your Spelling Dictionary. Then write the meaning that best fits each sentence.

1. The cat ran into the house.
2. The witch turned the prince into a frog.

Spelling and Writing

Do animals like warm, sunny days? Write three sentences to explain. Use list words such as *sunshine, everyone,* and *sometimes*. Revise and proofread your sentences.

Review and Extend

Checkup

Finish each word to make a compound word.

1. ___thing	4. ___plane
2. ___not	5. __self
3. __side	6. birth___

7. so__thing	10. in__
8. __metimes	11. every__e
9. ___shine	12. __body

Bonus Words

Write the bonus word that fits in each word shape.

1.

2.

3.

airplanes
birthdays
kites

Challenge Words Physical Education

Write the word for each clue.

1. a way of swimming
2. small house
3. area used to camp
4. a wiggly line
5. a class

campground
cabin
dogpaddle
course
zigzag

26 Vowel Sound in ball

Introduction

Focus These words have the vowel sound in **ball**.

- This vowel sound may be spelled **a, aw,** and **o**.

Say the Words

Listen for the vowel sound in *ball*. Notice how the sound is spelled in each word.

1.	all	7.	small
2.	call	8.	kickball
3.	fall	9.	draw
4.	saw	10.	crawl
5.	dog	11.	log
6.	walk	12.	because

Wild Words The words *walk* and *because* have the vowel sound in *ball*. Notice how each is spelled.

Practice the Words

1. Write the words from 1 to 6 that rhyme.
2. Write the words from 1 to 6 that mean "exercise" and "pet."
3. Write the word whose letters also spell *was*.
4. Write the words from 7 to 12 in alphabetical order.

Sum Up What did you learn about how the vowel sound in *ball* may be spelled?

For Extra Practice, see page 209.

all call fall saw dog walk

Change one letter to make a list word.

1. talk
2. say
3. ill
4. dig
5. wall
6. fell

small kickball draw crawl log because

Write the word for each clue.

7. firewood
8. game
9. why
10. creep
11. tiny
12. make a picture

Word Building

Listen for the **-all** in **call**. Add **-all** to make a new word.

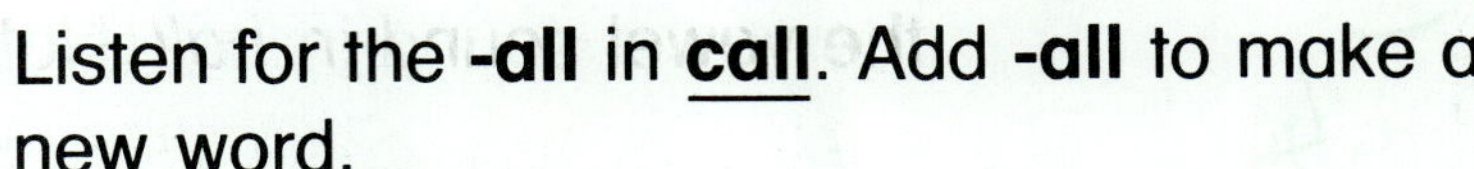

Listen for the **-alk** in **walk**. Add **-alk** to make a new word.

26 Application

all
call
fall
saw
dog
walk

small
kickball
draw
crawl
log
because

Spelling Connections

Spelling and Language Skills

Capitalization The first word in a sentence is always capitalized. The word **I** is also always capitalized.

My friend and I went to the store.

I bought bread and milk.

Proofreading Write each sentence correctly. Check for capital letters and spelling.

1. i sow Sue at the playground.
2. she and i played kikball.

Spelling and Handwriting Skills

Study the models of **f** and **b**. Both letters touch the top line. Write the letters carefully.

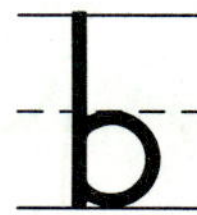

Spelling and Writing

These animals are friends. Write three sentences telling about things they do together. Use list words such as *walk, call,* and *crawl*. Revise and proofread your sentences.

Review and Extend

Checkup

Write a list word by adding the missing letters.

1. d_g	4. w_lk	7. bec__se	10. sm_ll
2. _ll	5. c_ll	8. dr__	11. cr__l
3. s__	6. f_ll	9. l_g	12. kickb_ll

Bonus Words

walking
wanted
calling
drawing

Write the bonus word for each clue.

1. going on foot
2. coloring
3. wished for
4. shouting

Challenge Words Science

goose
ostrich
chicken
robin
parrot

Write the words to finish the puzzle.

ACROSS

1. web-footed bird
4. talking bird
5. lays eggs we eat

DOWN

2. large bird that can't fly
3. has a red breast

27 Vowel Sounds with r

Introduction

Focus These words have the vowel sounds with **r** in **car** and **horn**.

- The vowel sound with **r** in **car** may be spelled **ar**.
- The vowel sound with **r** in **horn** may be spelled **or**.

Say the Words

Listen for the vowel sound with **r** in each word.

1. car	7. part
2. far	8. hard
3. start	9. farmyard
4. sport	10. store
5. more	11. short
6. orange	12. morning

Wild Words The words *orange* and *morning* have the vowel sound with **r** in *horn*.

Practice the Words

1. Write the words from 1 to 6 in alphabetical order.
2. Write the words from 7 to 12 in alphabetical order.
3. Underline the words with the vowel sound in *car*.

Sum Up What did you learn about how the vowel sounds with **r** in *car* and *horn* may be spelled?

More Practice

For Extra Practice, see page 210.

car far start sport more orange

Write the list word for each clue.

1. not near
2. auto
3. tennis or soccer
4. not less
5. a fruit or color
6. begin

part hard farmyard store short morning

Write the list word that begins and ends like each word.

7. mug
8. had
9. see
10. pot
11. food
12. sent

Word Building

Listen for the **-art** in **start**. Add **-art** to make a new word.

1. c ___ 2. sm ___

Listen for the **-ort** in **sport**. Add **-ort** to make a new word.

1. f ___ 2. p ___

27 Application

car
far
start
sport
more
orange

part
hard
farmyard
store
short
morning

Spelling Connections

Spelling and Thinking Skills

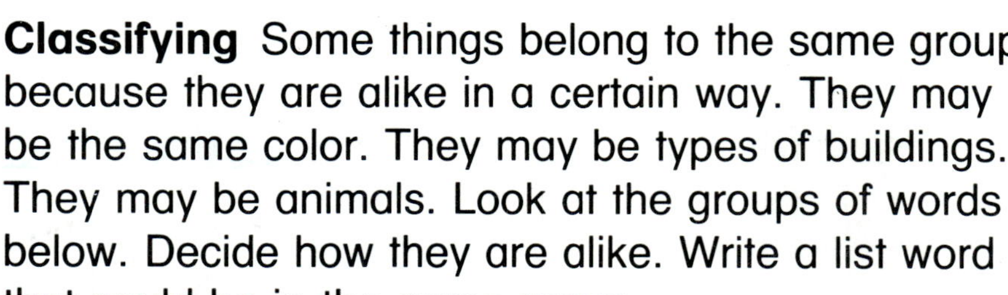

Classifying Some things belong to the same group because they are alike in a certain way. They may be the same color. They may be types of buildings. They may be animals. Look at the groups of words below. Decide how they are alike. Write a list word that could be in the same group.

1. bus
train
plane

2. apple
pear
cherry

3. afternoon
evening
noon

Spelling and Dictionary Skills

Word Meanings Many words have more than one meaning. Look up the word *part* in your Spelling Dictionary. Write the number of the definition that matches each sentence.

1. Mother made a part in my hair.
2. Ed only finished part of his homework.
3. The kitchen is one part of a house.

Spelling and Writing

Write three sentences about visiting a farm. Use list words such as *part, farmyard,* and *orange*. Revise and proofread your sentences.

Review and Extend

Checkup

Write a list word by adding the missing letters **ar** or **or**.

1. st__t	**4.** f__
2. m__e	**5.** __ange
3. c__	**6.** sp__t

7. m__ning	**10.** st__e
8. sh__t	**11.** h__d
9. f__myard	**12.** p__t

Bonus Words

or
for
are

Write the bonus word to finish each sentence.

1. This is ___ you.

2. I'll have milk ___ juice.

3. We ___ ready to go.

Challenge Words Language Arts

meaning
dictionary
homophones
action
poetry

Write the word to finish each sentence.

1. *Ate* and *eight* are ___.

2. Please look that word up in the ___.

3. Verbs are words that may show ___.

4. I like to read ___.

5. What is the ___ of that word?

28 Vowel Sound with r

Introduction

Focus These words have the vowel sound with **r** in **her**, **fur**, **word**, and **dirt**.

- This vowel sound with **r** may be spelled **er**, **ur**, **or**, and **ir**.

Say the Words

Listen for the vowel sound in *her*.

1. her
2. hurt
3. turn
4. work
5. girl
6. were
7. verb
8. burn
9. word
10. bird
11. stir
12. purple

Wild Words The words *were* and *purple* have the vowel sound in *her*. Notice how each is spelled. Don't forget the final **e** in *were*.

Practice the Words

1. Write the words with the vowel sound spelled **er** or **ur**.
2. Write the words with the vowel sound spelled **or** or **ir**.

Sum Up How may vowel sounds with **r** be spelled?

More Practice

For Extra Practice, see page 211.

her hurt turn work girl were

Write the list word to finish each sentence.

1. It's my ___ now.
2. Who is that ___?
3. Where ___ you?
4. I ___ my arm.
5. Sue found ___ book.
6. Dad left for ___.

verb burn word bird stir purple

Write a list word that belongs with each group.

1. green, blue, ___
2. sore, cut, ___
3. noun, pronoun, ___
4. sentence, letter, ___
5. bee, fly, ___
6. mix, beat, ___

Word Building

Listen for the **-ir** in **girl**. Add **-ir** to make a new word.

1. sw ___ l
2. tw ___ l

Listen for the **-or** in **work**. Add **-or** to make a new word.

1. c ___ k
2. f ___ k

Spelling Connections

her
hurt
turn
work
girl
were

verb
burn
word
bird
stir
purple

Spelling and Language Skills

Capitalization and Punctuation A **statement** begins with a **capital letter** and ends with a **period** [.].

We are going now.

A **question** begins with a **capital letter** and ends with a **question mark** [?].

Do you want a ride?

Proofreading Write each sentence correctly. Check for capital letters, punctuation, and spelling.

1. who is that gril.
2. she has a pirple dress

Spelling and Handwriting Skills

Study the models of **i** and **u**. Then write the letters. Remember to dot the **i**.

Spelling and Writing

Write three sentences about the job the rabbit has to do. Use list words such as *work, turn,* and *stir.* Revise and proofread your sentences.

Review and Extend

Checkup

Write a list word by adding the missing letters **er**, **ur**, **or**, or **ir**.

1. w__e
2. h__
3. h__t
4. g__l
5. w__k
6. t__n
7. st__
8. w__d
9. v__b
10. b__n
11. p__ple
12. b__d

Bonus Words

turning
turned
working
worked

Write the bonus word that fits in each word shape.

1. 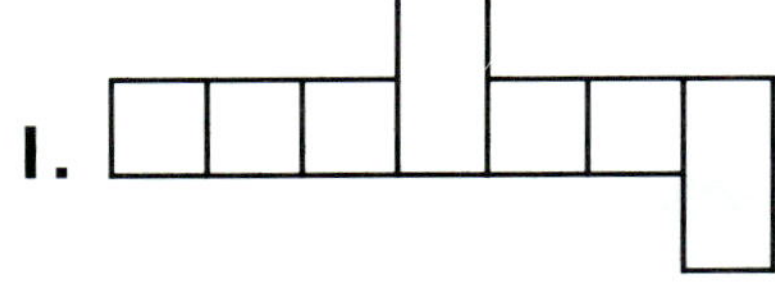

3. 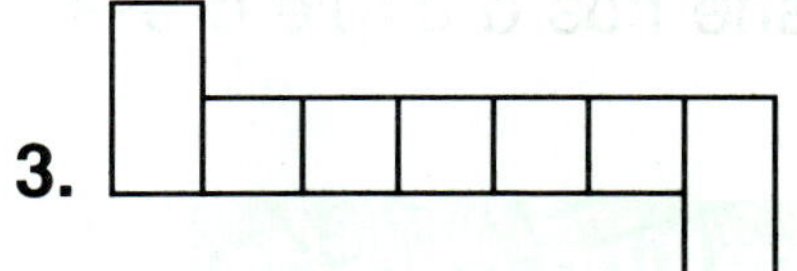

2. 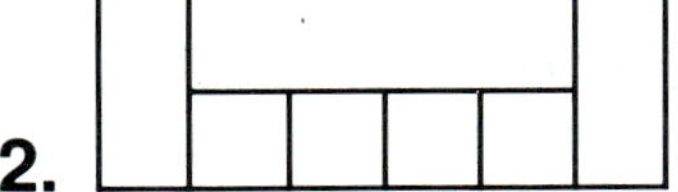

4. 

Challenge Words Reading

folk tale
tailor
peasant
soldier
beast

Write the words to finish the story.

My grandmother told me a (1). There was once a (2) boy who lived on a farm. He wanted to join the army and become a (3), but his family needed him to help protect the farm from a huge (4). The boy got the (5) to help him sew a huge trap. Now I can't remember how the story ended!

29 Sight Words

Introduction

Focus Some words are not spelled the way they sound. You must study the spelling of these words.

Say the Words

Notice how each word is spelled.

1. look	7. took
2. good	8. book
3. come	9. some
4. many	10. very
5. could	11. should
6. school	12. special

Wild Words Be careful when you say and write the words *school* and *special*. Notice how the sound /k/ is spelled in *school*. Notice how the end of *special* is spelled.

Practice the Words

1. Write the words with the **short e** sound.
2. Write the words with the vowel sound heard in *cook*.
3. Write the words that rhyme with *gum*.
4. Write the word that rhymes with *rule*.

Sum Up Why must these words be studied very carefully?

For Extra Practice, see page 212.

look good come many could school

Write the list word for each meaning.

1. place to learn
2. was able to
3. a number of
4. well done
5. see
6. get to a place

took book some very should special

Write the list word for each clue.

1. speck + ial − k =
2. silver + y − sil =
3. boo + ty + k − ty =
4. toot − t + k =
5. sh + would − w =
6. some + one − one =

Word Building

Listen for the **-ood** in **good**. Add **-ood** to make a new word.

1. w ___ 2. st ___

Listen for the **-ool** in **school**. Add **-ool** to make a new word.

1. p ___ 2. sp ___

Spelling Connections

look
good
come
many
could
school

took
book
some
very
should
special

Spelling and Thinking Skills

Inferences Look at the underlined words in the sentences below. They make no sense. Look for clues to the meaning of each word. Write the list word that belongs in the sentence.

1. I have two brothers. How flyx do you have?
2. I can't find my cat. Let's go blump for it.
3. I like ice cream. It tastes so slib.
4. I want to read. Where is my nurp?

Spelling and Dictionary Skills

Parts of an Entry A dictionary entry may have a picture to help you. Read the definitions below for *school*. Then write the letter of the picture that matches each definition.

1. a place for teaching and learning
2. the pupils and teachers of a school

a.

b.

Spelling and Writing

What would you teach these animals? Write three sentences to explain. Use list words such as *book, special,* and *school*. Revise and proofread your sentences.

Review and Extend

Checkup

Write a list word by adding the missing letters.

1. sch__l	4. c_m_	7. b__k	10. s_m_
2. m_n_	5. c__ld	8. v_r_	11. spec__l
3. g__d	6. l__k	9. t__k	12. sh__ld

Bonus Words

looking
looked
coming

Write the bonus word to finish each sentence.

1. When is Tom ___ home?
2. We have been ___ for him.
3. We even ___ in the park.

Challenge Words Science

heat
temperature
fog
wind
earthquake

Write the word to answer each question.

1. What blows the leaves?
2. What tells how warm or cold it is outside?
3. What do you need to make water boil?
4. What causes the ground to move?
5. What is like a cloud but near the ground?

30 Review

Spelling Strategy

Tracing Words Practice tracing a word to remember how it is spelled. First, write the word. Next, trace over it with your finger and say the word without looking at it. Then write the word again.

Activity Choose three words from Lesson 29. Practice tracing them. Then write the words.

Compound Words A compound word is made from two words that can be put together.

25

airplane **inside** **myself** **cannot** **birthday** **anything**

Write the words that begin with consonants.

1. ___ 2. ___ 3. ___

Write the list words by adding the missing vowels.

4. _ _rpl_n_ 5. _nyth_ng 6. _ns_d_

sunshine **nobody** **sometimes** **something** **into** **everyone**

Write the list words by adding the missing vowels.

7. s_nsh_n_ 9. _nt_ 11. s_m_t_m_s
8. _v_ry_n_ 10. s_m_th_ng 12. n_b_dy

Find the word *thing* in a list word.
Write the list word. 12a. ___

Vowel Sound in ball The vowel sound in **ball** may be spelled **a, aw,** and **o.**

26

all **call** **fall** **saw** **dog** **walk**

Write the list words that fit the clues.

shout	every one of	go on foot
1. ___	**2.** ___	**3.** ___

Write the list word that begins with the same letter and sound. Then circle the letter or letters that make the vowel sound in *ball.*

food	dad	set
4. ___	**5.** ___	**6.** ___

small **kickball** **draw** **crawl** **log** **because**

Change one letter to make a list word.

drew	smell	leg
7. ___	**8.** ___	**9.** ___

Write the list words to complete the sentences.

10. We came in ___ it was raining.
11. We played ___ after school.
12. Did you see the bug ___ up the wall?

Vowel Sounds with r The vowel sound with **r** in **car** may be spelled **ar.** The vowel sound with **r** in **horn** may be spelled **or.**

Write the words in alphabetical order. Then circle the letters that make a vowel sound with **r.**

27

car	**far**	**start**	**sport**	**more**	**orange**
1. ___		**3.** ___		**5.** ___	
2. ___		**4.** ___		**6.** ___	

part	**hard**	**farmyard**	**store**	**short**	**morning**
7. ___		**9.** ___		**11.** ___	
8. ___		**10.** ___		**12.** ___	

Vowel Sound with r The vowel sound with **r** in **her, fur, word,** and **dirt** may be spelled **er, ur, or,** and **ir.**

Write a list word that has a vowel sound with **r** by adding the missing letter or letters.

28

her	**turn**	**girl**
hurt	**work**	**were**

1. _ir_
2. _er
3. __rt
4. __rn
5. wo__
6. _er_

verb	**word**	**stir**
burn	**bird**	**purple**

7. _or_
8. _urpl_
9. _er_
10. _ir_
11. _ur_
12. __ir

Sight Words Some words are not spelled the way they sound. Look at them carefully.

29

look **good** **come** **many** **could** **school**

Write the list words that mean the opposite.

few bad go

1. ___ **2.** ___ **3.** ___

Write the list words that fit in the shapes.

4. ___ **5.** ___ **6.** ___

took **book** **some** **very** **should** **special**

Complete the sentences with list words.

7. I am not ___ tall.
8. The ___ for lunch today is pizza.
9. Will you get me ___ milk?

Write the two list words that rhyme.

10. ___ **11.** ___

Write the word that begins with **sh**. **12.** ___

Spelling Connections

Reading A Paragraph

In this lesson, you will write a paragraph about a friend or neighbor. A paragraph is a group of sentences that tells about a main idea. One sentence tells the main idea. The others tell about the main idea.

The paragraph below tells about someone who is a good neighbor to all of us. He is Eldon Muller. Mr. Muller's job is finding new foods to feed people in the future.

Eldon Muller works with vegetables and grains from all over the world. He works with wheat, corn, rice, and the winged bean. The winged bean is a vegetable that has more protein than almost any other vegetable. Protein is a food part the body needs. Protein helps the body grow and stay healthy. Mr. Muller feels almost certain the winged bean will be used in the future.

from "Two Good Neighbors" by
Charles David Raphael

Answer the question.
Which sentence tells the main idea?

1. Protein is a food part the body needs.
2. Eldon Muller works with vegetables and grains from all over the world.

Speaking and Listening

Think of a friend or neighbor to write about. Tell who the person is and something interesting you might write about that person.

Writing A Paragraph

Review Words

anything
start
more
her
work
were
look
good
many
could

Now you will write a paragraph to read to the class. Follow these steps.

Prewriting Draw a picture of your friend or neighbor. Make a list of ideas to write about. Choose spelling words you can use.

Writing Begin the first sentence of your paragraph a few spaces from the left. Write your main idea. Write other sentences that tell about the main idea.

Revising Does the first sentence of your paragraph begin a few spaces from the left? Do you have a main idea? Do the other sentences tell about the main idea? Are the review words spelled correctly? Use the checklists on pages 176 and 177.

Presenting Read your paragraph to the class. Let them ask questions about your friend or neighbor.

31 Contractions

Introduction

Focus A **contraction** is a shortened form of two words. An **apostrophe [']** takes the place of the missing letters.

Say the Words

Notice the apostrophe in each word.

1. don't
2. can't
3. isn't
4. we're
5. it's
6. I'll
7. hasn't
8. haven't
9. I've
10. I'm
11. you're
12. your

Wild Words The words *you're* and *your* sound alike, but have different spellings and meanings. *You're* is the contraction for "you are." *Your* means that something belongs to you.

Practice the Words

1. Write the words with the contraction for *not*.
2. Write the words with *it* and *I*.
3. Write the words that mean "we are," "you are," and "belonging to you."

Sum Up What did you learn about how contractions may be spelled?

More Practice

For Extra Practice, see page 213.

don't can't isn't we're it's I'll

Write the contraction that contains each word below.

1. I
2. do
3. we
4. can
5. is
6. it

hasn't haven't I've I'm you're your

Write the correct word to finish each sentence.

7. ___ been working.
8. ___ very tired.
9. I hope ___ coming with us.
10. Where is ___ bag?
11. Kim ___ arrived.
12. I ___ left yet.

Word Building

Listen for the **-n't** in **isn't**. Add **-n't** to make a new word.

1. are ___
2. would ___
3. was ___
4. should ___

Spelling Connections

don't
can't
isn't
we're
it's
I'll

hasn't
haven't
I've
I'm
you're
your

Spelling and Language Skills

Capitalization Special names for people, places, and animals are called **proper nouns**. Proper nouns begin with capital letters.

Meg and Mark live in San Francisco.

Proofreading Write each sentence correctly. Check for capital letters and spelling.

1. I'l visit jenny in Dallas.
2. Your flying to grand rapids.

Spelling and Handwriting Skills

Study the models of **o** and **a**. Then write the letters carefully.

Spelling and Writing

Imagine you are watching the parade. Write three sentences about it. Use list words such as *we're*, *it's*, and *I'm*. Revise and proofread your sentences.

Review and Extend

Checkup

Write a list word by adding the missing letter or letters.

1. _'ll	4. _an'_
2. _on'_	5. _e'r_
3. _t'_	6. __n'_

7. ___r	10. ___'re
8. _'m	11. ha_en'_
9. _'ve	12. __sn'_

Bonus Words

yellow
black
brown
blue

Write the bonus word to finish each sentence.

1. A zebra has ___ stripes.
2. A banana is ___.
3. The sky and sea are ___.
4. A sparrow has ___ feathers.

Challenge Words Mathematics

sixth
seventh
eighth
ninth
tenth

Write the word to finish each sentence.

1. The monkey is ___.
2. The zebra is ___.
3. The giraffe is ___.
4. The elephant is ___.
5. The lion is ___.

32 Ending Sound in baby

Introduction

Focus These words have the ending sound in **baby**.

- The ending sound in **baby** may be spelled **y**.

Say the Words

Listen for the ending sound.

1. funny
2. happy
3. party
4. story
5. baby
6. money
7. easy
8. pretty
9. silly
10. penny
11. lucky
12. cookie

Wild Words The words *money* and *cookie* have the ending sound in *baby*. Notice how the ending sound is spelled in each word.

Practice the Words

1. Write the words from 1 to 6 in alphabetical order.
2. Write the words from 7 to 12 in alphabetical order.

Sum Up What did you learn about how words with the ending sound in *baby* may be spelled?

More Practice

For Extra Practice, see page 214.

funny happy party story baby money

Write the list word that fits in each word shape.

1. 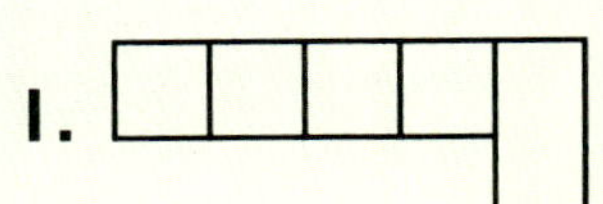
2. 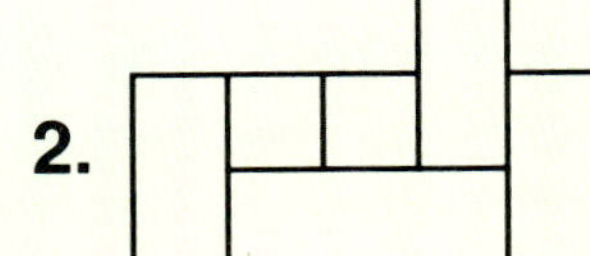
3. 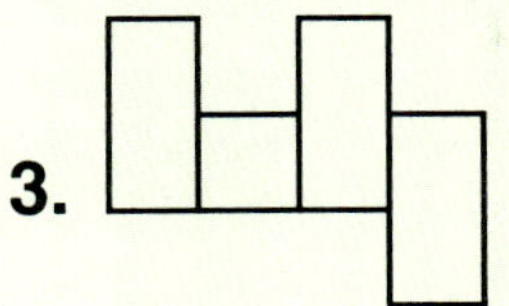
4. 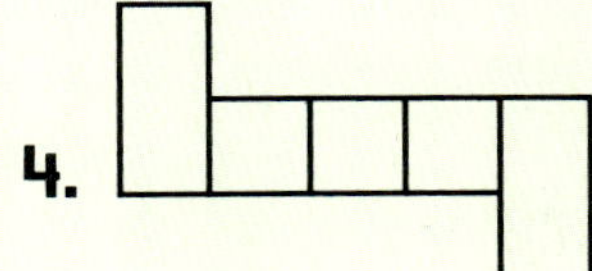
5. 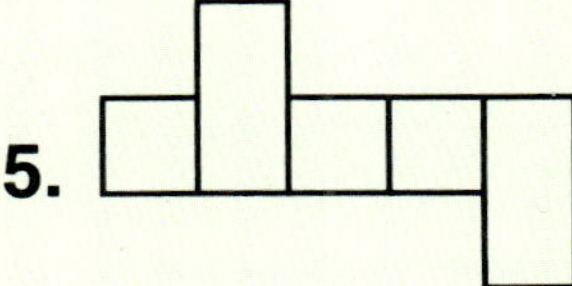
6. 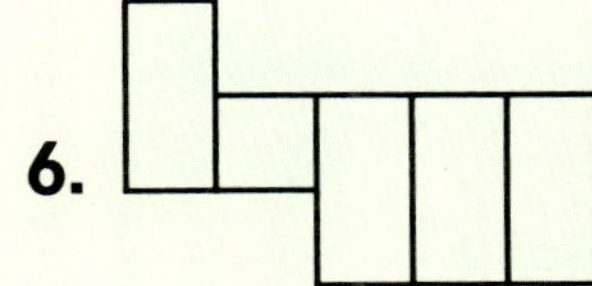

easy pretty silly penny lucky cookie

Write the list word for each clue.

7. a flat cake
8. funny
9. one cent
10. cute
11. not hard
12. having good luck

Word Building

Listen for the **-y** in **happy**. Add **-y** to make a new word.

1. rock ___
2. cloud ___
3. rain ___
4. cream ___

32 Application

funny
happy
party
story
baby
money

easy
pretty
silly
penny
lucky
cookie

Spelling Connections

Spelling and Language Skills

Capitalization The first word of a sentence and the pronoun **I** are always capitalized. A **statement** ends with a **period [.]**. A **question** ends with a **question mark [?]**.

Proofreading Write each sentence correctly. Check for capital letters, periods, question marks, and spelling.

1. i liked this storie
2. aren't the pictures pritee

Spelling and Handwriting Skills

Write the letters **e** and **l**. The **e** touches the middle line. The **l** touches the top line.

Spelling and Writing

What is the boy doing? Write three sentences to explain. Use list words such as *money*, *penny*, and *lucky*. Revise and proofread your sentences.

Review and Extend

Checkup

Write a list word by adding the missing letters.

1. ___ey	4. ___py	7. ____ty	10. ___ky
2. __by	5. ___ry	8. ___ny	11. __sy
3. ___ny	6. ___ty	9. ____ie	12. ___ly

Bonus Words

peek
crab
flat
flag

Write the bonus word that rhymes.

1. bag 2. grab 3. week 4. mat

Challenge Words Science

wilderness
quicksand
river
creek
ocean

Write the words to finish the puzzle.

DOWN
1. large body of salt water
3. small stream of water
4. large stream of water

ACROSS
2. sand in which things sink
5. an area where few people live

33 Adding -es

Introduction

Focus The ending **-es** can be added to some words to name more than one.

- If a word ends with a **consonant** and **y**, change the **y** to **i** and add **-es**.

Say the Words

Listen for the endings. Think about how the base word changes when you add *-es*.

1. sky
2. skies
3. fly
4. flies
5. puppy
6. puppies
7. candy
8. candies
9. lady
10. ladies
11. family
12. families

Wild Words Remember the **i** before the **l** in the words *family* and *families*.

Practice the Words

1. Write the words that end in **y**.
2. Write the words that rhyme with *prize*.
3. Write the words that rhyme with *please*.

Sum Up What did you learn about adding **-es** to base words ending with a **consonant** and **y**?

More Practice

For Extra Practice, see page 215.

sky skies fly flies puppy puppies

Follow the math clues. Write the list words.

1. pup + p + y =
2. s + fly − s =
3. pup + pies =
4. sky + ies − y =
5. sky + ies + y − iesy =
6. fly + ies − y =

candy candies lady ladies family families

Count the blanks. Write the list word to finish each phrase.

7. one _ _ _ _ _ _
8. two _ _ _ _ _ _ _ _
9. one _ _ _ _ _
10. two _ _ _ _ _ _ _
11. one _ _ _ _
12. two _ _ _ _ _ _

Word Study

Change the **y** to **i** and add **-es** to make a new word.

1. bunny
2. body
3. fry
4. cherry

Spelling Connections

sky
skies
fly
flies
puppy
puppies

candy
candies
lady
ladies
family
families

Spelling and Thinking Skills

Comparing The sentences below compare two different animals and how they move.

Example: A fish swims. A bird ___.
Answer: A fish swims. A bird *flies*.

Write the list word to finish each comparison.

1. A cat has kittens. A dog has ___.
2. Cars move on land. Planes move in the ___.

Spelling and Dictionary Skills

Parts of an Entry A **dictionary entry** includes the **definitions** and the **special forms** of a word. Use your Spelling Dictionary to answer these questions.

1. How many entries are there for *fly*[2]?
2. What are all the special forms for *fly*[2]?
3. What is the fourth definition for *fly*[2]?

Spelling and Writing

What are the people in the picture doing? Write three sentences. Use list words such as *sky*, *family*, and *puppy*. Revise and proofread your sentences.

Review and Extend

Checkup

Write a list word by adding the missing letters.

1. _l_	4. _k__s
2. __pp_	5. _l__s
3. _k_	6. pupp___

7. cand___	10. __d_
8. fami__	11. __nd_
9. lad___	12. famili__

Bonus Words

Write a bonus word for each base word.

1. story 2. cry 3. baby 4. try

cries
tries
babies
stories

Challenge Words School Subjects

Write the word for each meaning.

1. learning about numbers
2. learning about insects and plants
3. learning to spell and write
4. learning how to take care of yourself
5. studying people and their ways

Science
Language
Social Studies
Health
Mathematics

34 Words That Sound Alike

Introduction

Focus Some words sound alike, but they have different spellings and meanings.

Say the Words

Listen to the words that sound alike. Think about the spelling and meaning of each set of words.

1. here
2. hear
3. for
4. four
5. one
6. won
7. two
8. to
9. too
10. there
11. their
12. they're

Wild Words Learn when to use *there*, *their*, and *they're*. *There* tells you where something is. *Their* tells you who owns something. *They're* is a contraction for *they are*.

Practice the Words

1. Write the words starting with letters **a** to **f**.
2. Write the words starting with letters **g** to **l**.
3. Write the word starting with letters **m** to **s**.
4. Write the words starting with letters **t** to **z**.

Sum Up What did you learn about how words that sound alike may be spelled?

 For Extra Practice, see page 216.

here hear for four one won

Write the list word to finish each sentence.

1. I can't ___ you.
2. Come over ___.
3. Dan has ___ sisters.
4. This is ___ them.
5. Alice ___ a prize.
6. I won ___ too.

two to too there their they're

Write the list word for each clue.

7. also
8. one + one
9. Bob's and Al's
10. not here
11. toward
12. they are

Word Study

Add **-ee** and **-ea** to make pairs of words that sound alike.

1. s ___
2. s ___
3. w ___ k
4. w ___ k

Spelling Connections

here
hear
for
four
one
won

two
to
too
there
their
they're

Spelling and Thinking Skills

Classifying Words can tell you many things. Some words tell **where**. Some words tell **how many**. Some words tell **what** someone can do or may have done. Complete the chart with list words.

where	how many	what
near	many	run
far	two	jumped

Spelling and Dictionary Skills

Word Meanings Read the definitions for *two*, *to*, and *too* in your Spelling Dictionary. Write the correct word to finish each sentence.

1. I have ___ much work.
2. Give some ___ Jim.
3. One and one are ___.
4. Jane wants to go ___.

Spelling and Writing

Write three sentences about winning a game. Use list words such as *four*, *they're*, and *won*. Revise and proofread your sentences.

Review and Extend

Checkup

Write a list word by adding the missing letter or letters.

1. w_n	4. f_r
2. o_e	5. h_r_
3. f__r	6. h__r

7. _w_	10. th__'re
8. t__	11. th_r_
9. t_	12. th__r

Bonus Words

be
bee
by
buy

Write the bonus word that fits each word shape.

1. 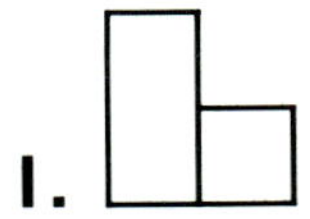 2. 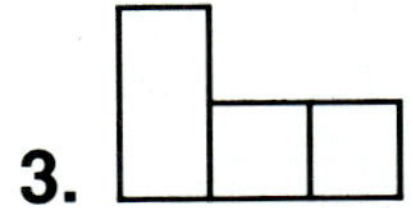 3. 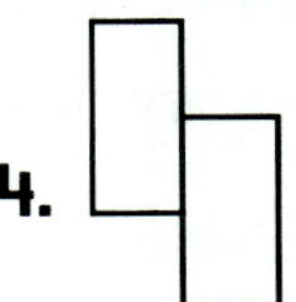 4.

Challenge Words Science

observe
investigate
compare
model
adult

Write the word for each meaning.

ACROSS
1. a small copy
3. to ask questions about
5. find how things are alike

DOWN
2. look at closely
4. a grown-up

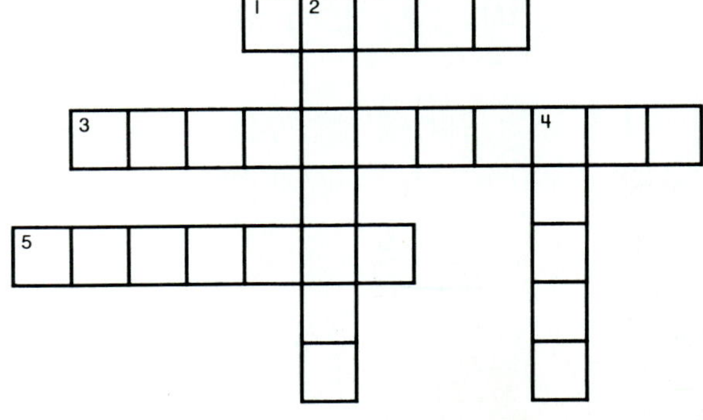

Introduction

Vowel Sound with r

Focus These words have the vowel sound with **r** at the end of **flower**.

- This vowel sound with **r** may be spelled **er**.

Say the Words

Listen for the vowel sound with **r**.

1. mother	7. under
2. father	8. over
3. sister	9. water
4. brother	10. after
5. flower	11. teacher
6. answer	12. another

Wild Words Remember to write the **w** in *answer*. The two words *an* and *other* form the word *another*.

Practice the Words

1. Write the words that begin with a vowel.
2. Write the words that name people.
3. Write the words that name things.

Sum Up What did you learn about how the vowel sound with **r** in *flower* may be spelled?

More Practice

For Extra Practice, see page 217.

mother father sister brother flower answer

Write the list word that begins and ends like each word.

1. flatter
2. sir
3. far
4. bear
5. air
6. muffler

under over water after teacher another

Write the list words to finish the story.

It is twenty minutes (7) two. School will soon be (8). We have (9) ten minutes. Our (10) is standing (11) the flag. Joe will (12) the plants before we go.

Word Building

Listen for the **-er** in **sister**. Add **-er** to make a new word.

1. play ___
2. paint ___
3. hamm ___
4. wint ___

35 Application

mother
father
sister
brother
flower
answer

under
over
water
after
teacher
another

Spelling Connections

Spelling and Language Skills

Capitalization Begin the names of days, months, and holidays with capital letters.

Mother's Day is a Sunday in May.

Proofreading Read the sentences. Check for capital letters and spelling. Then write the sentences correctly.

1. I gave dad a flowr on father's day.
2. He put it in woter on monday.

Spelling and Handwriting Skills

Study the models of **v** and **w**. Then write the letters carefully.

Spelling and Writing

Imagine you are at the circus. Write three sentences telling about it. Use list words such as *water*, *over*, and *under*. Revise and proofread your sentences.

Review and Extend

Checkup

Write a list word by adding the missing letters.

1. flow__	4. fath__
2. broth__	5. moth__
3. answ__	6. sist__

7. anoth__	10. wat__
8. aft__	11. und__
9. ov__	12. teach__

Bonus Words

game
games
stone
stones

Use the underlined letters to write bonus words.

1. Is that clown wearing spats?
2. I see the orange wig.
3. His huge earmuffs are like fuzzy balloons.
4. His giant shoes make him trip.

Challenge Words Reading

dangerous
detective
secret
escape
search

Write the words to finish the story.

LOST: ONE LION The circus is in town. The owner has hired a _(1)_. Lions can be _(2)_, and one did _(3)_ from the circus. This can't be a _(4)_. The _(5)_ is on.

36 Review

Spelling Strategy

Check Your Spelling Sometimes you may not be sure how to spell a word. Try writing the word. Does it look correct to you? If it doesn't, try writing the word another way. Often you will be able to see which of the spellings is correct.

Activity Which word in each pair is spelled correctly? Check the word list.

1. storey, story 2. silly, sillie 3. flys, flies

Contractions An apostrophe takes the place of the missing letters in a contraction.

Write the words that begin with **i.** Then write the words that begin with consonants. Circle each apostrophe and the letter or letters after it.

31

don't **can't** **isn't** **we're** **it's** **I'll**

1. ___
2. ___
3. ___
4. ___
5. ___
6. ___

hasn't **haven't** **I've** **I'm** **you're** **your**

7. ___
8. ___
9. ___
10. ___
11. ___
12. ___

Ending Sound in baby The ending sound in **bab<u>y</u>** may be spelled **y.**

32

funny **happy** **party** **story** **baby** **money**

Write the list word that begins with the same sound.

bat	fish	men
1. ___	**3.** ___	**5.** ___
pet	hand	stop
2. ___	**4.** ___	**6.** ___

Write the word for each clue. Circle the letter that makes the ending sound in *baby.*

glad	a book or tale	a birthday group
6a. ___	**6b.** ___	**6c.** ___

easy **pretty** **silly** **penny** **lucky** **cookie**

Study the words. Cover them. Write the words you can remember. Then write the rest of the words. Circle the letter or letters that make the ending sound in *baby.*

7. ___	**9.** ___	**11.** ___
8. ___	**10.** ___	**12.** ___

Write the list word with the consonant sound /k/ spelled **ck**.

12a. ___

Adding -es To name more than one if the word ends with a consonant and **y,** change the **y** to **i** and add **-es.**

Write the list words by adding the missing letters.

33

sky **fly** **puppy**
skies **flies** **puppies**

1. p_____s
2. s_y
3. f___s
4. s___s
5. p___y
6. f_y

candy **lady** **family**
candies **ladies** **families**

7. c_____s
8. l____s
9. f____y
10. f______s
11. c___y
12. l__y

Words That Sound Alike Some words that sound alike have different spellings and meanings.

34

here **hear** **for** **four** **one** **won**

Write the list words by adding the missing letters.

1. f__ 2. __n 3. h__e 4. _e_r

Write the two words for numbers.

5. ___ 6. ___

two **to** **too** **there** **their** **they're**

Write the list words by adding the missing letters.

7. t__r_
8. t___'re
9. tw_
10. _o
11. t___r
12. _o_

Vowel Sound with r The vowel sound with **r** at the end of **flower** may be spelled **er.**

35

mother **father** **sister** **brother** **flower** **answer**

Use the clues to write list words. Circle the letters **er.**

a rose is one
1. ___

goes with a question
2. ___

a dad
3. ___

Write the two list words that rhyme.

4. ___ **5.** ___

Write the longer word for *sis*. **6.** ___

under **over** **water** **after** **teacher** **another**

Write the list words that fit the clues. Circle the letters **er.**

person at school
7. ___

something to drink
8. ___

opposite of *before*
9. ___

Write the list words to complete the sentences.

10. Please have ___ apple.
11. Your fork fell ___ the table.
12. We will go ___ to Rob's house.

Spelling Connections

Reading A Book Report

Can you think of a book in which the characters do something clever? In this lesson you will write a book report telling what some clever story characters do. Use paragraph form.

You may know a book called *The Bremen-Town Musicians.* It is about four clever animals. They scared away a band of robbers. Read what the animals did.

The four friends thought of a way to get rid of the robbers. The donkey put his front legs on the window. The dog jumped on the donkey's back. The cat climbed up on the dog. The rooster perched on the cat.

Then they all made their music in their loudest voices. The donkey brayed, the dog barked, the cat gave out a cry, and the rooster crowed.

from *The Bremen-Town Musicians,* Retold and Illustrated by Ilse Plume

Answer the question.
Why was the way the animals scared the robbers clever?

Speaking and Listening

Talk about a story such as "Jack and the Beanstalk" in which the characters do something clever. Tell what the characters do that is clever.

Writing A Book Report

Write a book report to share with the class. Use paragraph form. Follow these steps.

Prewriting Write the title and author of your book. List things the characters do that are clever. List spelling words you can use.

Writing Write the book title and author. Underline the title. Write the rest of your report in paragraph form. For each paragraph, write a sentence that tells the main idea. Tell how the characters in your book are clever.

Revising Did you tell how the characters are clever? Did you begin each paragraph a few spaces from the left? Did you spell the review words correctly? Use the checklists on pages 176 and 177.

Presenting Work in small groups. Read your book report to the group. You may want to draw a picture to illustrate your report.

Review Words

don't
can't
it's
I'll
funny
happy
here
for
won
answer

Word Study

A. Words with **Short a, e, and i**
Lessons 1, 2, 3

Short a	**Short e**	**Short i**
dad	get	did

Which word has the same vowel sound as the first word? Write the word.

Example:

sit   last   lift   rest   lift

1. hen   plant   miss   nest
2. six   still   best   glass
3. can   ten   grass   trick

B. Words with **Short o and u**   Lessons 4, 5

Short o	**Short u**
got	fun

Which word has the same vowel sound as the first word? Write the word.

Example: top   run   but   job   job

1. mom   shot   push   pull
2. bug   block   skunk   trot

Note: If you need to look up any words in Word Study, use the *Scott, Foresman Beginning Dictionary.*

C. Words Beginning with **cl, dr, sm, st, sw**

Lesson 9

cl	**dr**	**sm**	**st**	**sw**
class	**dr**ess	**sm**ell	**st**op	**sw**im

1. Write the word that begins with **sm**.
   snowed smash simple
2. Write the word that begins with **dr**.
   driven dirty doorway
3. Write the word that begins with **sw**.
   sunny sawed sweater
4. Write the word that begins with **cl**.
   colder clever caller

D. Words Ending with **mp, nd, nt, sk, st**

Lesson 10

mp	**nd**	**nt**	**sk**	**st**
ju**mp**	e**nd**	we**nt**	a**sk**	ju**st**

1. Write the word that ends with **nt**.
   find note mint
2. Write the word that ends with **sk**.
   rest risk tracks
3. Write the word that ends with **mp**.
   blame maps damp
4. Write the word that ends with **nd**.
   stand hunt garden

E. Words Beginning with **ch, sh, th, wh**
Lesson 11

ch	**sh**	**th**	**wh**
chin	**sh**all	**th**at	**wh**en

1. Write the word that begins with **th**.
   tomato thankful hitter
2. Write the word that begins with **ch**.
   cheap close cashed
3. Write the word that begins with **wh**.
   wearing however whimper
4. Write the word that begins with **sh**.
   school shark skirt

F. Words Ending with **ch, sh, th, ng**
Lesson 13

ch	**sh**	**th**	**ng**
mu**ch**	fi**sh**	ba**th**	thi**ng**

1. Write the word that ends with **ng**.
   stony wagon strong
2. Write the word that ends with **ch**.
   fresh touch tooth
3. Write the word that ends with **th**.
   tonight mouth sight
4. Write the word that ends with **sh**.
   smash cloths dusk

G. Words with **Long a, e, i, and o**
Lessons 14, 15, 16, 17, 19

Long a	m**a**k**e**	r**ai**n	w**ay**	
Long e	k**ee**p	**ea**t	sh**e**	
Long i	t**i**m**e**	k**i**nd	cr**y**	r**igh**t
Long o	th**o**s**e**	m**o**st	g**oa**t	sh**ow**

Which word has the same vowel sound as the first word? Write the word.

Example: try green high play — high

1. each might throw speak
2. hold broke steam grind
3. mail treat brave tight

H. Vowel Sound in **moon** Lesson 20

Vowel Sound in moon

f**oo**d n**ew**

Which word has the same vowel sound as *moon?* Write the word.

Example: tool boat old — tool

1. only shampoo plain
2. grew know please

I. Adding -s and -es Lesson 21

Add *-s* to most words.
boy → boys swing → swings

Add *-es* to a word ending in **ch, sh,** or **x.**
lunch → lunches fox → foxes

Add *-s* or *-es* to each word.

Example: box boxes

1. brush

2. tax

3. march

4. pencil

J. Adding -ing and -ed Lesson 23

Some words end with one vowel followed by one consonant. Double the last consonant and add *-ing* or *-ed*.
hop → hopping hop → hopped

Add *-ing* or *-ed* to each word.

Example: bat + ed batted

1. win + ing

2. grab + ed

3. trip + ing

4. star + ed

K. Vowel Sound in **ball** Lesson 26

Vowel Sound in ball

all **aw** **o**

all saw dog

Which word has the same vowel sound as *ball?* Write the word.

Example: goat full draw draw

1. pull always bell
2. shall still hog

L. Vowel Sounds with r Lessons 27, 28

car	sport	her
start	corn	hurt
		work
		girl

Which word has the same vowel sound as the first word? Write the word.

Example: hard morning purple farmyard farmyard

1. turn explore turtle charge
2. short charm words score
3. part harmless before thirsty

Commonly Misspelled Words

again
always
answer
because
been
before
can't
coming
didn't
don't
February
first
for
friend
guess
hear
here
him
it's
just
knew
know
little
many
morning
mother
much
off
once
our
people
pretty
said
school
some
something
sometimes
that's
their
then
there
they
they're
thought
to
together
too
until
very
went
were
when
where
won't
would
you're

Revising and Proofreading Checklist

After you write something, look at what you wrote. Ask yourself questions like the ones below. Use the proofreading marks on the next page to show changes you want to make.

Content

- ✓ Did I say what I wanted to say?
- ✓ Will my descriptions help others to see what I am writing about?
- ✓ Did I give enough information?
- ✓ Are my directions clear enough for someone else to follow?

Mechanics

- ✓ Did I spell words correctly?
- ✓ Do all my sentences begin with capital letters?
- ✓ Do I have a period (**.**) or a question mark (**?**) at the end of each sentence?

Proofreading Marks

Mark	Meaning
≡	Make a capital letter.
∧	Add a word or words.
ℓ	Take out a word or words.
(sp)	Correct the spelling.
⊙	Add a period.

Example

Fishing Fun

We went fishing at Frog Lake. dad caught four fishes ~~at Frog Lake~~. Mom cought one. My brother Rusty ~~he~~ caught twoe. I did not catch any We all had fun.

Glossary of Terms

alphabet An alphabet is the letters of a language. The letters of the English alphabet are *a, b, c, d, e, f, g, h, i, j, k, l, m, n, o, p, q, r, s, t, u, v, w, x, y,* and *z*.

alphabetical order Alphabetical order is words arranged by letters in the order of the alphabet. For example, the words *and, bed, cat,* and *day* are in alphabetical order.

apostrophe An apostrophe is a mark (') used in contractions to show that one or more letters have been left out. For example, the apostrophe in *isn't* shows that a letter has been left out. *Isn't* is the contraction for *is not*. The letter that has been left out is the letter *o*.

compound word A compound word is two words that are put together to make another word. For example, the compound word *birthday* is made up of the words *birth* and *day*.

consonant A consonant is a letter of the alphabet that is not a vowel. Consonants in the English language are the letters *b, c, d, f, g, h, j, k, l, m, n, p, q, r, s, t, v, w, x, y,* and *z*.

consonant sound A consonant sound is a sound that may be spelled by one or more consonant letters. For example, in the word *neck*, the sound /k/ is spelled *ck*.

contraction A contraction is a shortened form of two words. It uses an apostrophe to take the place of the missing letters. For example, the contraction *haven't* is a shortened form of the words *have not*. The apostrophe in *haven't* takes the place of the missing letter *o*.

dictionary A dictionary is a book that explains the words of a language. For an example of a dictionary, see pages 231–280.

ending An ending is the letter *-s* or the letters *-es, -ed, -ing, -er,* and *-est,* which may be added to the end of a word. For example, the word *boxes* is made up of the word *box* and the ending *-es*.

entry An entry in a dictionary is a word you look up and everything written about the word. For an example of an entry, see page 230.

entry word An entry word is a word explained in a dictionary. It appears in heavy type and shows how it may be divided in writing. For an example of an entry word, see page 230.

guide words Guide words are the two words in dark type at the top of a dictionary page. The first guide word is the first entry word on the page. The second guide word is the last entry word on the page. Other entries on the page appear in alphabetical order between the guide words. For example, the guide words on page 231 are *a* and *another*.

inference An inference is a good guess or a conclusion. For example, if you know the meaning of the word *flag*, you may make the inference that a *flagpole* is a pole for flying a flag.

noun A noun is a word that names a person, place, or thing. For example, the words *brother, school,* and *flower* are nouns.

period A period is a dot (.) marking the end of a sentence that is a statement. For example, the following sentence is a statement and ends with a period. *The baby is happy.*

proper noun A proper noun is a special name for a person or animal. Proper nouns always begin with capital letters. For example, *Jack* is a proper noun.

question A question is a sentence that asks something. For example, the following sentence is a question. *Where is Ana?*

question mark A question mark is a mark (?) that comes at the end of a question. For example, the following sentence is a question and ends with a question mark. *Is this your hat?*

sentence A sentence is a group of words that tells a complete idea. For example, the following words make a sentence. *The boy saw a fox.*

special form A special form is a word in dark type at the end of a dictionary entry. Usually a special form is the entry word with the letters *-s, -es, -ed, -ing, -er,* or *-est* added to it. For example, the words *looks, looked,* and *looking* are special forms for the entry word *look*. Some special forms may change the spelling of the entry word. For example, the entry word *fly* has the special forms *flies, flew, flown,* and *flying*.

statement A statement is a sentence that tells something. A statement begins with a capital letter and ends with a period. For example, the following sentence is a statement. *A duck can swim.*

vowel Vowels are the letters *a, e, i, o, u,* and sometimes *y*.

vowel sound A vowel sound is a sound that one or more vowels may stand for. For example, the vowels *ea* may stand for the long vowel sound /ē/ heard in the word *eat*.

Spelling Concepts

Some words have the **short a** sound in **cat**. 1
- **Short a** may be spelled **a**.

Some words have the **short e** sound in **pen**. 2
- **Short e** may be spelled **e**.

Some words have the **short i** sound in **pin**. 3
- **Short i** may be spelled **i**.

Some words have the **short o** sound in **pot**. 4
- **Short o** may be spelled **o**.

Some words have the **short u** sound in **cup**. 5
- **Short u** may be spelled **u**.

Some words have the consonant sound in **car**, **kite**, 7
and **black**. This consonant sound may be spelled **c**, **k**, and **ck**.

Some consonant sounds are spelled with two letters 8
that are the same.

Some words begin with two consonants pronounced 9
together.

clock **drum** **small** **star** **swing**

10 Some words end with consonants pronounced together.

lamp **bend** **tent** **mask** **test**

11 Some consonant sounds are made by two letters pronounced as one.

chair **shoe** **thing** **white**

13 Some ending sounds are made by two letters pronounced as one.

such **dish** **path** **wing**

14 Many words with a long vowel sound are spelled with **vowel-consonant-e**.

save **nine** **pole**

15 Some words have the **long a** sound in **pail** and **day**. **Long a** may be spelled **ai** and **ay**.

16 Some words have the **long e** sound in **bee**, **sea**, and **he**.

- **Long e** may be spelled **ee**, **ea**, and **e**.

17 Some words have the **long i** sound in **kind**, **sky**, and **might**.

- **Long i** may be spelled **i**, **y**, and **igh**.

19

Some words have the **long o** sound in **no**, **coat**, and **slow**.

- **Long o** may be spelled **o**, **oa**, and **ow**.

20

Some words have the vowel sound in **moon**.

- The vowel sound /ü/ as in **moon** may be spelled **oo** and **ew**.

21

The endings **-s** and **-es** can give a word the added meaning "more than one."

- Add **-s** to most words.
- Add **-es** to words that end in **ch**, **sh**, and **x**.

22

The endings **-ing** and **-ed** are added to many words.

- If a word ends in **e**, drop the **e** and add **-ing** or **-ed**.

23

The endings **-ing** and **-ed** are added to many words.

- Some words end with one vowel followed by one consonant as **hop** and **bat** do. With words like these, double the final consonant and add **-ing** or **-ed**.

25

A **compound word** is two words that are put together to make another word.

play + ground = playground

26 Some words have the vowel sound in **ball**.

- This vowel sound may be spelled **a**, **aw**, and **o**.

27 Some words have the vowel sounds with **r** in **car** and **horn**.

- The vowel sound with **r** in **car** may be spelled **ar**.
- The vowel sound with **r** in **horn** may be spelled **or**.

28 Some words have the vowel sound with **r** in **her**, **fur**, **word**, and **dirt**.

- This vowel sound with **r** may be spelled **er**, **ur**, **or**, and **ir**.

29 Some words are not spelled the way they sound. You must study the spelling of these words.

31 A **contraction** is a shortened form of two words. An **apostrophe** (') takes the place of the missing letters.

32 Some words have the ending sound in **baby**.

- The ending sound in **baby** may be spelled **y**.

The ending **-es** can be added to some words to name more than one.

- If a word ends with a **consonant** and **y**, change the **y** to **i** and add **-es**.

33

Some words sound alike, but they have different spellings and meanings.

34

Some words have the vowel sound with **r** at the end of **flower**.

- This vowel sound with **r** may be spelled **er**.

35

Words with **Short a**

dad **had** **pat** **can** **has** **have**

Read the sentences below. Write the missing list words.

My friend __(1)__ a dog. I like to __(2)__ the dog on its head. My __(3)__ said I __(4)__ __(5)__ a dog too. My dad __(6)__ a dog when he was a boy.

1. ___
2. ___
3. ___
4. ___
5. ___
6. ___

bad **sat** **tag** **man** **ran** **half**

Write the list word that goes with each pair of words.

woman, child
7. ___

third, whole
8. ___

jumped, hopped
9. ___

stood, kneeled
10. ___

touch, tap
11. ___

glad, sad
12. ___

Words with **Short e**

ten **men** **get** **red** **yes** **said**

Use the code. Put a letter in place of each number. Write the list word.

1	2	3	4	5	6	7	8	9	10	11
m	g	r	t	e	n	d	y	s	a	i

9 + 10 + 11 + 7

1. ___

2 + 5 + 4

2. ___

1 + 5 + 6

3. ___

4 + 5 + 6

4. ___

8 + 5 + 9

5. ___

3 + 5 + 7

6. ___

met **let** **set** **hen** **pen** **seven**

Write each list word that ends with **en**. Then circle the letter that makes the **short e** sound.

7. ___ **8.** ___ **9.** ___

Write each list word that rhymes with *get*. Then circle the letter that makes the **short e** sound.

10. ___ **11.** ___ **12.** ___

3

Words with **Short i**

his **did** **six** **him** **if** **give**

Write the list word that answers each riddle.

It begins with **h**. It rhymes with *swim*.

1. ___

It begins with **d**. It rhymes with *hid*.

2. ___

It begins with **s**. It rhymes with *mix*.

3. ___

Find the list word hidden in each word below. Write the list word.

wife **4.** ___

forgiven **5.** ___

history **6.** ___

sit **bit** **tip** **dig** **big** **been**

Write the list word that begins and ends like each clue word.

boon **7.** ___
bat **8.** ___
top **9.** ___
bag **10.** ___
sat **11.** ___
dog **12.** ___

4

Words with **Short o**

got **lot** **hot** **box** **mom** **gone**

Follow the clues. Write each list word.

g + once − c ma − a + om b + sox − s

1. ___ **2.** ___ **3.** ___

Write the list words that end in **ot**.

4. ___ **5.** ___ **6.** ___

job **top** **hop** **spot** **doll** **upon**

Use the clues to write the list words.

rhymes with *hot* a toy that spins to move on one foot

7. ___ **8.** ___ **9.** ___

There is a musical note where each vowel belongs in the words below. Decide which vowels are missing. Then write the list words.

j♪b d♪ll ♪p♪n

10. ___ **11.** ___ **12.** ___

Write the list word that is made up of two two-letter words. **12a.** ___

5

Words with **Short u**

fun **run** **sun** **but** **bug** **was**

Write a list word to complete each riddle.

Add an **s** to **un**. You can sit in the ___.

Add an **r** to **un**. You can begin to ___.

Add an **f** to **un**. You will have ___.

1. ___ **2.** ___ **3.** ___

Write the list words that complete this sentence.

The b___ w___ big, b___ I was bigger.

4. ___ **5.** ___ **6.** ___

bus **gum** **mud** **rug** **nut** **once**

Write the list word that matches each clue.

rain, slush — car, train — twice, three times

7. ___ **8.** ___ **9.** ___

Write the list word that rhymes with each word.

sum — bug — but

10. ___ **11.** ___ **12.** ___

7

Words with **c, k,** and **ck**

cup **kid** **back** **duck** **sock** **kitten**

Write the list word that matches each clue.

shoe, slipper	baby, puppy	bowl, plate
1. ___	**2.** ___	**3.** ___

Follow the clues. Write each list word.

barn − rn + ck	kite − te + d	dull − ll + ck
4. ___	**5.** ___	**6.** ___

neck **kick** **sick** **pick** **rock** **picnic**

Choose a list word to complete each sentence clue. Then write the list words to complete the puzzle.

DOWN

7. How many apples did you ___?

8. We bought food for the ___.

9. He can ___ the ball far.

ACROSS

10. The opposite of *well* is ___.

11. I wore a scarf around my ___.

12. She threw a ___ into the water.

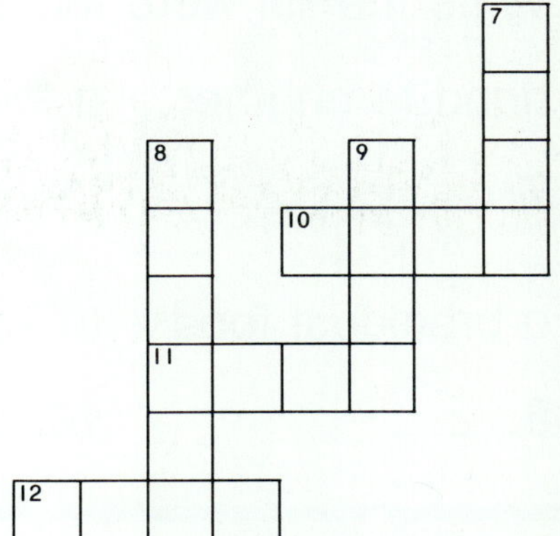

8

Words with Two Consonants

well **hill** **miss** **off** **add** **guess**

Each clue word below contains a list word. Write the list word. Circle the two letters that are the same.

offer	address	swell
1. ___	**2.** ___	**3.** ___

Change one letter in each word to make a list word. Write the list word.

hall	mist	guest
4. ___	**5.** ___	**6.** ___

bell **tell** **will** **pass** **egg** **rabbit**

Write the list word that matches each clue.

hand to another	a thing that rings	animal with long ears
7. ___	**9.** ___	**11.** ___
a breakfast food	to say	is going to
8. ___	**10.** ___	**12.** ___

9

Words Beginning with **cl, dr, sm, st, sw**

class **dress** **smell** **stop** **swim** **climb**

Each group of letters in the puzzle is part of a list word. Write the list words by adding the missing letters. The letters in the circles will spell a word. The word answers this riddle: *What does a group of letters do to a word?*

1. ◯_ell
2. sto ◯
3. dr ◯ss
4. _ ◯imb
5. c ◯_ss
6. ◯_im

clap **clock** **drag** **step** **swell** **clothes**

Look at the underlined letters in each word below. Write the list word that has the same letters.

start	**7.** ___	swish	**10.** ___
doctor	**8.** ___	drop	**11.** ___
plan	**9.** ___	other	**12.** ___

10

Words Ending with **mp, nd, nt, sk, st**

jump **end** **went** **ask** **just** **friend**

Write the list word hidden in each sentence.

1. He will bend the branch from the tree.
2. She believes in justice for all people.
3. She likes to wear jumpers to school.
4. They all wore masks to the surprise party.
5. They know that friendship is important.
6. There were twenty questions on the test.

stamp **hand** **land** **desk** **must** **different**

Write the list word that completes each sentence.

7. She looks ___ today.
8. All the papers are on the ___.
9. He ___ take the test.
10. He held a pencil in his ___.
11. The plane will ___ soon.
12. I put a ___ on the letter.

7. ___
8. ___
9. ___
10. ___
11. ___
12. ___

11

Words Beginning with **ch, sh, th, wh**

chin **shall** **them** **then** **when** **what**

Follow the clues. Write each list word.

where − re + n	ship − ip + all	thank − ank + em
1. ___	**3.** ___	**5.** ___
their − ir + n	chip − p + n	whale − ale + at
2. ___	**4.** ___	**6.** ___

check **shop** **shell** **thick** **where** **wear**

Read the clues. Then write the list words to complete the puzzle.

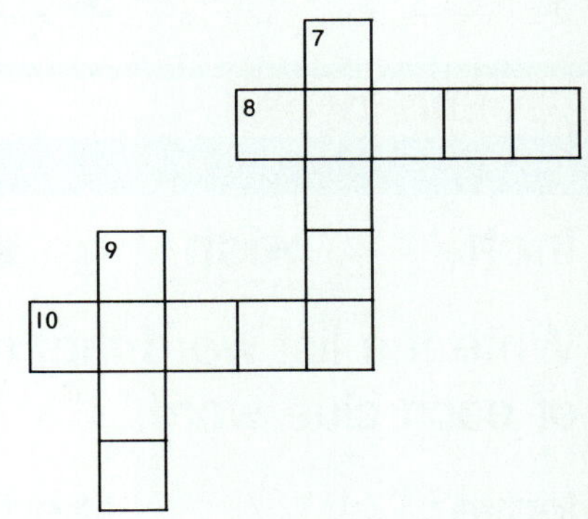

DOWN

7. to make a mark

9. to go to the store and buy

ACROSS

8. the cover of a turtle

10. the opposite of *thin*

Write the two list words that sound alike but have different meanings.

11. ___ **12.** ___

13

Words Ending with **ch, sh, th, ng**

much **which** **fish** **bath** **thing** **think**

Read the clues. Then write the list words to complete the puzzle.

DOWN
1. animal that swims
2. a lot

ACROSS
3. word ending in **ch**

Write the list word that rhymes with each clue word.

math	ring	drink
4. ___	**5.** ___	**6.** ___

inch **wish** **sing** **bring** **long** **nothing**

Write the list word that means the opposite of each clue word.

leave	short	everything
7. ___	**8.** ___	**9.** ___

Write the list word that completes each sentence.

She didn't move an ___.	I ___ she could go.	She will ___ a song.
10. ___	**11.** ___	**12.** ___

14

Words with **Vowel-Consonant-e**

make **take** **time** **five** **home** **please**

Write the list word that answers each riddle.

It begins with **f.**
It rhymes with
dive.

1. ___

It begins with **t.**
It rhymes with
lake.

2. ___

It begins with **p.**
It rhymes with
tease.

3. ___

Write the list word that matches each clue.

place to live,
house

4. ___

build,
put together

5. ___

minutes,
hours

6. ___

made **gave** **white** **whole** **those** **surprise**

Read the sentences below. Write the missing list words.

We **(7)** the school a **(8)**. The **(9)** class **(10)** a snowman. We put a cowboy hat on its **(11)** head. All **(12)** who saw it began to laugh.

7. ___
8. ___
9. ___
10. ___
11. ___
12. ___

15

Words with **Long a**

rain **mail** **way** **may** **play** **they**

Use the code. Put a letter in place of each number. Write the list word.

1	2	3	4	5	6	7	8	9	10	11	12
e	r	a	h	y	t	n	p	m	i	l	w

9 + 3 + 5
1. ___

2 + 3 + 10 + 7
2. ___

8 + 11 + 3 + 5
3. ___

6 + 4 + 1 + 5
4. ___

9 + 3 + 10 + 11
5. ___

12 + 3 + 5
6. ___

wait **train** **plain** **paint** **stay** **eight**

Add the missing letter to each word to write a list word.

wit
7. ___

rain
8. ___

plan
9. ___

Use the clues to write a list word.

make a picture
10. ___

a number word
11. ___

hold back
12. ___

16

Words with **Long e**

keep **feel** **read** **eat** **she** **three**

Write the list word hidden in each word below.

beating	shell	bread
1. ___	**2.** ___	**3.** ___

Write a list word that completes each sentence.

I have ___ puppies.	You may ___ the pen.	They ___ happy today.
4. ___	**5.** ___	**6.** ___

teeth **green** **team** **mean** **each** **between**

Write the list word that completes each sentence.

7. The lion looked ___ when it opened its mouth.
8. The fans cheered when the ___ scored.
9. He sat ___ Mom and Dad at the show.
10. The grass looked very ___ after the rain.
11. The dentist cleaned Joe's ___.
12. She gave a gift to ___ of us.

7. ___	**9.** ___	**11.** ___
8. ___	**10.** ___	**12.** ___

17

Words with **Long i**

find **kind** **cry** **try** **right** **eyes**

Write list words that rhyme with these words.

fly	mind	might
1. ___	**3.** ___	**5.** ___
2. ___	**4.** ___	

Write the word that begins with a vowel.

6. ___

mind **why** **high** **light** **night** **behind**

Write the list word that means the opposite of each clue word.

day	dark	low
7. ___	**9.** ___	**11.** ___
disobey	ahead	
8. ___	**10.** ___	

Write the word in which **long i** is spelled **y.**

12. ___

19

Words with **Long o**

most **told** **goat** **boat** **show** **know**

Change one letter in each word to make a list word. Write the list word.

gold
1. ___

post
2. ___

beat
3. ___

knob
4. ___

shop
5. ___

goal
6. ___

hold **old** **both** **grow** **own** **only**

There is a musical note where each vowel belongs in the words below. Decide which vowels are missing. Then write the list words.

b♪th **7.** ___
♪nly **8.** ___
h♪ld **9.** ___
♪ld **10.** ___
♪wn **11.** ___
gr♪w **12.** ___

20

Vowel Sound in **moon**

food **soon** **room** **tool** **new** **who**

Follow the clues. Write each list word.

n + few − f	root − t + m	flood − l
1. ___	**3.** ___	**5.** ___
so + one − e	what − at + o	stool − s
2. ___	**4.** ___	**6.** ___

cool **moon** **zoo** **flew** **chew** **knew**

The list words below are written in code. In the code *a* = *c*, *b* = *e*, *c* = *f*, and so on. Write the list words.

a	b	c	d	e	f	g	h	i	j	k
c	e	f	h	k	l	m	n	o	w	z

giih	ehbj	aiif
7. ___	**9.** ___	**11.** ___
cfbj	adbj	kii
8. ___	**10.** ___	**12.** ___

21

Adding **-s** and **-es**

boys **lunches** **branches** **wishes** **foxes** **people**

Write the list word that has the same group of letters underlined in each word below.

purple	toy	punch
1. ___	**3.** ___	**5.** ___
can	shell	box
2. ___	**4.** ___	**6.** ___

Write the plural list word that does not end in **s** or **es**. **6a.** ___

swings **inches** **dishes** **bushes** **boxes** **children**

Write the list word that completes each group.

slides and	adults and	trees and
7. ___	**9.** ___	**11.** ___
bags and	feet and	pans and
8. ___	**10.** ___	**12.** ___

Write the plural list word that does not end in **s** or **es**. **12a.** ___

22

Adding **-ing** and **-ed**

liking **liked** **smiling** **smiled** **making** **hiding**

Write list words that rhyme with these words.

taking	filed	piling
1. ___	**3.** ___	**5.** ___
biking	riding	hiked
2. ___	**4.** ___	**6.** ___

racing **raced** **using** **used** **catching** **caught**

Write list words to complete the sentences.

7. Are you ___ a cold?
8. The cars are ___ fast.
9. Are you ___ that chair?
10. I ___ up all my paper.
11. She quickly ___ home.
12. Gina ___ the ball.

23

Adding **-ing** and **-ed**

hopping **hopped** **batting** **batted** **planning** **planned**

Write the two list words formed from each base word.

bat	hop	plan
1. ___	**3.** ___	**5.** ___
2. ___	**4.** ___	**6.** ___

napping **napped** **sledding** **sledded** **beginning** **began**

Follow the clues. Write each list word.

nap + p + ed	begin − in + an	sled + d + ed
7. ___	**8.** ___	**9.** ___

Read the sentences below. Write the missing list words.

At the **(10)** of the day we were wide awake. We went **(11)** in the park for four hours. By noon, Mom found us **(12)** in our room.

10. ___ **11.** ___ **12.** ___

25

Compound Words

airplane **inside** **myself** **cannot** **birthday** **anything**

Match each word in Column A to the right word in Column B to make a list word. Write the list word.

	A	+	B
1.	in		plane
2.	can		self
3.	birth		not
4.	any		day
5.	air		thing
6.	my		side

1. ___ **3.** ___ **5.** ___
2. ___ **4.** ___ **6.** ___

sunshine **nobody** **sometimes** **something** **into** **everyone**

Write the words that begin with vowels. Then write the words that begin with consonants.

7. ___ **9.** ___ **11.** ___
8. ___ **10.** ___ **12.** ___

Write the word that tells about weather.

12a. ___

26

Vowel Sound in **ball**

all **call** **fall** **saw** **dog** **walk**

Write the list words that rhyme.

1. ___ 2. ___ 3. ___

Write the list words that complete the sentence.

I (4) Jeff and his (5) (6) past the school.

4. ___ 5. ___ 6. ___

small **kickball** **draw** **crawl** **log** **because**

Follow the clues. Write the list word.

drape − pe + w

7. ___

smart − rt + ll

8. ___

frog − fr + l

9. ___

kicked − ed + ball

10. ___

became − me + use

11. ___

crayon − yon + wl

12. ___

Write three list words that have the sound /k/.

12a. ___ 12b. ___ 12c. ___

27

Vowel Sounds with **r**

car **far** **start** **sport** **more** **orange**

Add or subtract one letter in each word to make a list word. Write the list word.

star	farm	range
1. ___	**3.** ___	**5.** ___
scar	port	ore
2. ___	**4.** ___	**6.** ___

Write the word that begins with a vowel. **6a.** ___

part **hard** **farmyard** **store** **short** **morning**

Write the list word that matches each clue.

barn	piece	shop
7. ___	**8.** ___	**9.** ___

Write the list word that means the opposite of each clue word.

long	evening	easy
10. ___	**11.** ___	**12.** ___

Vowel Sound with **r**

her **hurt** **turn** **work** **girl** **were**

Write the list word that begins and ends like each clue word.

hit
1. ___

taken
2. ___

waste
3. ___

gill
4. ___

hammer
5. ___

walk
6. ___

verb **burn** **word** **bird** **stir** **purple**

The list words below are written in code. In the code each letter stands for the letter below it. Write the list word.

a	b	c	d	e	f	g	h	i	j	k	l	m	n
b	d	e	i	l	n	o	p	r	s	t	u	v	w

alif
7. ___

jkdi
8. ___

hlihec
9. ___

ngib
10. ___

mcia
11. ___

adib
12. ___

29

Sight Words

look **good** **come** **many** **could** **school**

Write the words that have the vowels **oo.**

1. ___ **2.** ___ **3.** ___

Write the words that complete the sentence.

How **(4)** children **(5)** **(6)** to the party?

4. ___ **5.** ___ **6.** ___

Write the word that rhymes with *pool.* **6a.** ___

took **book** **some** **very** **should** **special**

Write the list words that have the same beginning sounds as the clue words.

shake vase summer

7. ___ **9.** ___ **11.** ___

box tool space

8. ___ **10.** ___ **12.** ___

31

Contractions

don't **can't** **isn't** **we're** **it's** **I'll**

Write a contraction for the underlined word or words in each sentence.

1. I cannot find my pencil.
2. It is not in my desk.
3. I do not know where to look.
4. I will ask Joe to help.
5. I know it is here somewhere.
6. If we are lucky, we will find it.

1. ___ **3.** ___ **5.** ___
2. ___ **4.** ___ **6.** ___

hasn't **haven't** **I've** **I'm** **you're** **your**

Use each clue to write two list words.

words that sound alike	words with *I*	contractions with *not*
7. ___	**9.** ___	**11.** ___
8. ___	**10.** ___	**12.** ___

Write the word that is not a contraction.

12a. ___

32

Ending Sound in **baby**

funny **happy** **party** **story** **baby** **money**

Write the list words in alphabetical order. Circle the letter or letters that make the ending sound in *baby*.

1. ___ **3.** ___ **5.** ___
2. ___ **4.** ___ **6.** ___

Write the two list words that rhyme with *honey*.

6a. ___ **6b.** ___

easy **pretty** **silly** **penny** **lucky** **cookie**

Write three list words with double consonants.

7. ___ **8.** ___ **9.** ___

Write two list words with the sound /k/.

10. ___ **11.** ___

Write the list word that begins with a vowel. **12.** ___

33

Adding **-es**

sky **skies** **fly** **flies** **puppy** **puppies**

Write list words to complete the poem.

The bird **(1)** high
Up into the **(2)**.

The **(3)** are so blue
I'd like to **(4)** too.

1. ___
2. ___
3. ___
4. ___

Write list words to complete the sentences.

We watched the three **(5)** playing.
I chose the brown and white **(6)**.

5. ___
6. ___

candy **candies** **lady** **ladies** **family** **families**

Write the list words that contain the words below. Then circle the words that mean more than one.

am

7. ___
8. ___

ad

9. ___
10. ___

an

11. ___
12. ___

34

Words That Sound Alike

here **hear** **for** **four** **one** **won**

Find the list word hidden in each word below.
Write the list word.

reform	where	honey
1. ___	**3.** ___	**5.** ___
wonderful	fourteen	heart
2. ___	**4.** ___	**6.** ___

two **to** **too** **there** **their** **they're**

Read the sentences below. Write the missing list words.

The **(7)** boys are going **(8)** town. When they get **(9)**, **(10)** going to buy **(11)** mother a gift. They hope it won't cost **(12)** much.

7. ___	**9.** ___	**11.** ___
8. ___	**10.** ___	**12.** ___

35

Vowel Sound with **r**

mother **father** **sister** **brother** **flower** **answer**

Change the first letter to make a list word.

mister	bother	rather
1. ___	**2.** ___	**3.** ___

Write the list word that completes each group.

question and	plant and	sister and
4. ___	**5.** ___	**6.** ___

under **over** **water** **after** **teacher** **another**

Follow the clues. Write each list word.

rafter − r	later − l + w	ran − r + other
7. ___	**9.** ___	**11.** ___
thunder − th	preacher − pr + t	cover − c
8. ___	**10.** ___	**12.** ___

Write the list word that means the opposite of *over*. **12a.** ___

Review Test Lesson 6 List Words 1–6

Find the word in each group that is spelled correctly.

Sample					*Answer*
	men	menn	min	mene	men
1.	have	haf	hav	haff	
2.	tene	ten	tenn	tenne	
3.	sics	sixs	siks	six	
4.	gone	gonne	gunn	gon	
5.	sonn	suhn	sun	sunn	
6.	hot	hott	hatt	hote	
7.	redde	redd	rehed	red	
8.	hazz	haz	has	hase	

Review Test Lesson 6 List Words 7-12

9.	halv	half	haf	haph
10.	been	bin	binn	benne
11.	tipp	typ	tip	tippe
12.	jobe	job	joob	jobb
13.	wonce	onse	wonse	once
14.	sevan	sevven	sevin	seven
15.	set	sette	sett	sete
16.	mann	manne	man	mahn
17.	gumme	gum	gumm	guhm

Review Test Lesson 12 List Words 1–6

Find the underlined word that is spelled correctly.

Sample			*Answer*
	jomp over gump down	jump up jumb rope	jump
1.	to smeel the flowers to smel sweet	to smehl nice to smell good	
2.	wat and where wot I did	what if no matter whut	
3.	to ask a question to esk her	to askt me to axk him	
4.	a cute citten the little kitten	gray ketten silly kittin	
5.	to fall owf got aff	to turn off running awf	
6.	to gues right to gess the answer	trying to guez to guess who	
7.	a new freind best friend	make a frand an old frend	
8.	shall have shal be done	schall go today never shahl	

Review Test Lesson 12 List Words 7–12

9.	to pik up to pick flowers	to pic a partner to pyck the team
10.	know whair they are tell whaer to find it	where to go go wher I want
11.	to wear a dress to waer shoes	to wair well to whear a hat
12.	a nice stamb lick a stamp	penny stahmp save a stemp
13.	boil an eg break an egge	hard-boiled ege an egg and toast
14.	drage down dragg your feet	drag behind drahg a stick
15.	a cold swimm a fast suimm	a short suim a long swim
16.	rabbit hole white rabit	rabbot hutch rabitt ear
17.	school dessk roll-top desck	to sit at a desc teacher's desk

Review Test Lesson 18 List Words 1–6

Find the word in each group that is misspelled.

Sample					*Answer*
	right	home	rain	fich	fich
1.	way	five	wich	much	
2.	thrie	keep	think	may	
3.	bath	play	try	maile	
4.	they	eyez	time	cry	
5.	make	kind	finde	she	
6.	eat	pleeze	feel	think	
7.	tayke	thing	keep	rain	
8.	home	bath	readd	much	

Review Test   Lesson 18   List Words 7–12

9.	innch	team	night	feel
10.	long	think	trane	play
11.	beehind	time	light	teeth
12.	plain	grene	bath	sing
13.	high	wish	stay	whyte
14.	nothing	surprize	why	wait
15.	those	between	painte	made
16.	whole	each	gave	minde
17.	bringe	eight	right	mean

Review Test Lesson 24 List Words 1–6

Find the word that is spelled correctly to complete each sentence.

Sample					*Answer*
	The ___ were covered with snow.				
	branchez	brannches	branches	branchis	branches
1.	The ___ ate the grass.				
	gote	goat	goate	goute	
2.	I put the ___ back in the box.				
	tull	tooll	tool	toole	
3.	The rabbit ___ away.				
	hopd	hopped	hoppet	hoppt	
4.	I am ___ a snowman.				
	making	makking	makeing	mayking	
5.	Some ___ like baseball.				
	peepal	peopal	people	peeple	
6.	We will be there ___.				
	suun	soone	sune	soon	
7.	I ___ your picture.				
	lyked	liked	likte	liket	
8.	I ___ how to get there.				
	knoe	kno	noe	know	

9. Water helps flowers ___.
   gro grow groue growe

10. The baby ___ to cry.
   beegan begann began beggan

11. The dog ___ by the big chair.
   naped knapped napped nappt

12. I am ___ that pot for the soup.
   using eweing yousing useing

13. We told the ___ a story.
   chuldren childeren childrun children

14. I ___ you would win.
   knew noo knu nue

15. Please ___ the glass with two hands.
   holled wholed hold holld

16. We helped Dad wash the ___.
   dishas dishez diches dishes

17. You see the ___ at night.
   moon muun mune moone

Review Test Lesson 30 List Words 1–6

Find the word that is spelled correctly to complete each group of words.

Sample					*Answer*
	happy ___				
	burthday	birthday	berthday	birthdai	birthday
1.	a ___ bus				
	skool	schoole	scool	school	
2.	too ___ away				
	far	farr	fahr	farre	
3.	___ stop				
	canot	cannot	cannott	canott	
4.	a ___ time				
	goode	good	gud	guud	
5.	a long ___				
	wauk	wauke	wawk	walk	
6.	flying in an ___				
	ayrplane	airplane	arplane	areplain	
7.	___ my foot				
	hert	hurt	hirt	hirrt	
8.	a hard day at ___				
	work	wurk	wirk	werk	

Review Test Lesson 30 List Words 7–12

9.	laugh ___			
	sumtimes	sometymes	sumtymes	sometimes
10.	good ___			
	mawrning	morening	morning	morneng
11.	spelling the ___			
	word	werd	wurd	wird
12.	a ___ day			
	speshal	speshle	speshul	special
13.	to ___ around			
	craul	krawl	crawl	crall
14.	to ___ the soup			
	ster	stur	stir	sturr
15.	went ___ the water			
	intoo	intwo	inntoo	into
16.	playing ___			
	kikball	kickball	kikcball	kickbal
17.	toy ___			
	store	stor	staur	staure

Review Test Lesson 36 List Words 1–6

Find the underlined word that is misspelled.

Sample			*Answer*
	the blue skye a good story	a funny face a big baby	skye
1.	where itt's found blue skies	a lot of money a cute puppy	
2.	the fly buzzing many flies	little puppys my mother	
3.	a pink flowir her father	an older brother gave an answer	
4.	and don't go wone of those	but we're big over here	
5.	to hear a song for a while	wonn the prize four years old	
6.	with my father and we can't	and I'll come the birthday partty	
7.	my baby sistir dark skies	isn't sick my little brother	
8.	a happy day kant go	a toy for a baby making up a story	

Review Test Lesson 36 List Words 7–12

9.	a silly joke a pretty cat	a lucky friend anuther day
10.	hasn't gone yet if I'm leaving	a new peny sweet candy
11.	eating candies a nice ladey	all the families under the water
12.	three ladys a good teacher	after lunch going to eat
13.	for a minute four friends	the wrong answer havent been there
14.	your cat owver the hill	but you're going very easy work
15.	going to a party one cookey	up there hearing a story
16.	twoe cars they're saying	their house deep water
17.	a nice family four days	tooe many frogs won the game

Spelling Dictionary

Look at the dictionary entry below. Each part of the entry is labeled. This sample entry will help you when you look up a word in the Spelling Dictionary.

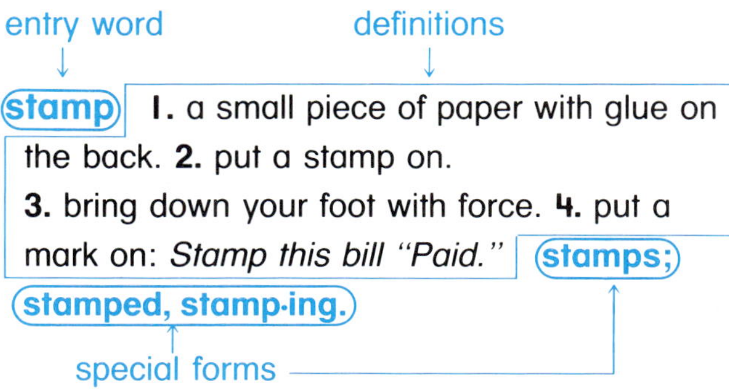

A a

a **1.** any: *Is there a book for me?* **2.** one: *Here is a pen.* **3.** each: *Flag Day comes once a year.*

ac tion **1.** doing something: *The quick action of the firemen saved the building from being burned down.* **2.** something done; act: *Giving the dog food was a kind action.* **3.** fast movement: *There is a lot of action in a basketball game.* **ac tions.**

action 3.

add **1.** put together: *Add 5 and 3 to make 8.* **2.** **Add to** means put with: *Dad added milk to the batter.* **add ed, add ing.**

ad di tion **1.** the adding of one number to another: *2 + 3 = 5 is a simple addition.* **2.** adding one thing to another: *The addition of flour will thicken gravy.* **ad di tions.**

a dult **1.** full-grown; grown-up; having full size and strength: *an adult person.* **2.** a grown-up person. **a dults.**

af ter **1.** later in time: *After school we'll go.* **2.** later; following: *The picnic came after the ball game.*

air plane a flying machine driven by propellers or jet engines. **air planes.**

airplane

all **1.** the whole of: *We ate all the cake.* **2.** every one of: *All these books are funny.* **3.** everyone: *All of us are going.*

am *I am here. I am going to be late. I am glad.*

an **1.** any: *Is there an orange in the dish?* **2.** one: *He is an inch taller than I am.* **3.** each: *She earns fifty cents an hour for baby-sitting.*

an oth er **1.** one more: *Eat another apple.* **2.** not the same; different: *Here's another picture.* **3.** a different one: *I don't like that song; sing me another.*

an swer 1. speak or act after someone asks a question: *He didn't answer my question.* **2.** words or action after someone asks a question: *Her answer was "no."* **3.** words or action to end a problem or a puzzle: *What is the correct answer to this puzzle?* **an swered, an swer ing; an swers.**

an y thing 1. any thing: *Do you have anything to eat?* **2.** at all: *My bike isn't anything like yours.*

are *We are here. You are my friend. You are all my friends. They are coming.*

ask 1. try to find out by words: *Why don't you ask the way?* **2.** look for the answer to: *Ask questions if you don't know.* **asked, ask ing.**

astronaut

as tro naut a member of the crew of a spaceship. **as tro nauts.**

at 1. *At* is used to show where: *Mother is at work.* **2.** *At* is used to show when: *Bill goes to bed at eight o'clock.*

aunt your father's sister or your mother's sister or your uncle's wife. **aunts.**

B b

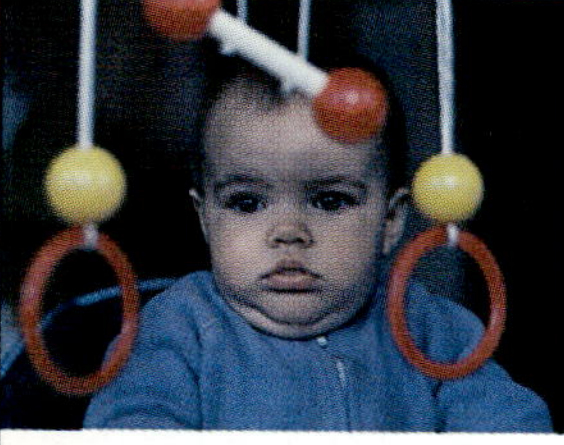
baby 1.

ba by 1. a very young child. **2.** for a baby: *baby shoes.* **3.** young or small: *baby chickens.* **ba bies.**

back 1. the part of your body opposite the front. **2.** the side of anything away from you: *the back of the picture.* **3.** part of a chair that a person leans against when sitting down. **4.** move away from the front: *He backed his car slowly.* **backs; backed, back ing.**

bad **1.** not good; not as it ought to be: *Teasing animals is a bad habit.* **2.** sorry: *I feel bad about being late for the parade.* **3.** sick: *I felt bad after eating that candy.* **worse, worst.**

bak er a person who makes or sells bread, pies, and cakes. **bak ers.**

ba nan a **1.** a fruit that grows in large bunches. **2.** the tree it grows on. **ba nan as.**

bat **1.** a thick stick or club, used to hit a ball. **2.** hit with a bat. **bats; bat ted, bat ting.**

bat 1.

bath a washing of the body: *I took a bath last night.* **baths.**

be *Can you be here all day? She tries to be on time. They will be hungry. He will be an athlete some day.* **be ing.**

beast any four-footed animal. *In stories, a beast is usually a fierce, cruel animal.* **beasts.**

be cause for the reason that; since: *Pat called us in because supper was ready.*

bed **1.** anything to sleep or rest on. **2.** a piece of ground in which plants are grown: *The flower bed is beautiful.* **beds.**

bee an insect that has four wings and often stings. *Bees make honey.* **bees.**

bees and flowers

been *This boy has been here for hours. The books have been read by everyone. We have been friends for years.*

be gan See **begin.** *He began to sing.*

be gin **1.** do the first part; start: *The party will begin soon.* **2.** start to be or happen: *The storm began yesterday.* **be gan, be gun, be gin ning.**

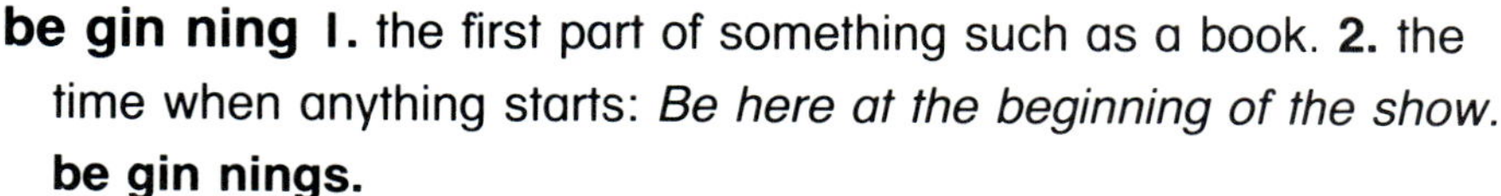

be gin ning **1.** the first part of something such as a book. **2.** the time when anything starts: *Be here at the beginning of the show.* **be gin nings.**

be hind **1.** at the back of: *Who is behind me?* **2.** not on time; late: *Her class is behind in its work.*

bell a hollow object, usually made of metal, shaped like a cup, that makes a ringing sound when struck by another piece of metal inside it. **bells.**

bell

be tween in the space or time from one thing to another: *There is a rock between two trees. We'll be home between two and three o'clock.*

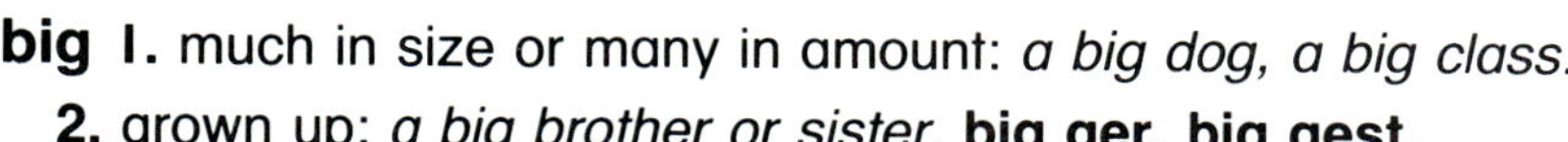

big **1.** much in size or many in amount: *a big dog, a big class.* **2.** grown up: *a big brother or sister.* **big ger, big gest.**

bike a bicycle. **bikes.**

bird an animal that has wings and feathers. Most birds can fly. **birds.**

birth day the day on which a person was born. **birth days.**

bit See **bite.** *He bit into the candy bar.*

bite **1.** cut with the teeth: *Did she bite her tongue?* **2.** the amount you bite off: *I ate only a bite of my apple.* **3.** a sore made by biting or stinging. **bit, bit ten** or **bit, bit ing; bites.**

a **bite** of watermelon

black **1.** the opposite of white; the color of coal. **2.** without light; very dark: *Without a moon the night was black.* **blacks.**

block **1.** a thick piece of wood or other material. **2.** fill so nothing can pass by: *The car was blocking traffic.* **3.** a square of land: *We walked around the block.* **blocks; blocked, block ing.**

blue **1.** the color of the clear sky during the day. **2.** having this color. **blues; blu er, blu est.**

boat a vehicle that floats on water and can be moved by motor, by sail, or by oars. **boats.**

book written or printed sheets of paper bound together.

bor row get something from a person to use for a short time: *He has borrowed my book.* **bor rowed, bor row ing.**

both **1.** the one and the other: *Both houses are pink.* **2.** the two together: *Both dogs are mine.*

box a container, or case, made of wood, metal, paper, or cardboard to put things in. **box es.**

boy a male child. **boys.**

branch **1.** a part of a tree that grows out from the trunk. **2.** one part of something that is divided: *The river divides into two branches.* **branch es.**

bring come with something from another place: *Please bring me a napkin.* **brought, bring ing.**

broth er a boy with the same parents as another. **broth ers.**

brown **1.** a dark color like that of toast or coffee. **2.** having that color: *Many horses are brown.* **browns; brown er, brown est.**

buf fa lo a large animal with a shaggy head. American buffaloes are called bison. **buf fa loes, buf fa los,** or **buf fa lo.**

buffalo

bug a crawling or a flying insect. **bugs.**

bu gle a musical instrument that you play by blowing into it. **bu gles.**

burn **1.** be on fire; be very hot. **2.** set on fire: *Please burn the trash.* **3.** a sore caused by heat: *She got a burn on her arm from the hot iron.* **burned** or **burnt, burn ing; burns.**

bus a large automobile that carries passengers along certain streets or roads. **bus es.**

bus

bush a plant smaller than a tree, with many branches starting from or near the ground. **bush es.**

but **1.** on the other hand: *You may go, but you may not stay late.* **2.** except: *The restaurant is open every day but Monday.*

buy get by paying for: *You can buy a pencil for school. We bought a new car.* **bought, buy ing.**

by **1.** near; beside: *Stand by the door.* **2.** making use of: *He travels by bus.* **3.** not later than: *Be here by twelve o'clock.*

C c

building a log **cabin**

cab in **1.** a small house: *a log cabin.* **2.** a place for passengers in an airplane or ship. **cab ins.**

cal en dar a table or chart showing the months, weeks, and days of the year. **cal en dars.**

call **1.** speak loudly; cry; shout: *He called for help.* **2.** telephone to: *Call me when you get home.* **called, call ing.**

came See **come.** *Dad came home early.*

camp ground place for camping. **campgrounds.**

can[1] **1.** be able to: *She can run fast.* **2.** know how to: *She can read.* **3.** have the right to: *Anyone can enter the contest.* **could.**

can[2] **1.** a container of metal or glass. **2.** keep by sealing tightly: *Did your aunt can some peaches?* **cans; canned, can ning.**

can dy sugar or syrup, boiled with water and flavoring, then cooled and made into small pieces for eating. **can dies.**

can not can not: *I cannot sing very well.*

can't cannot.

cap i tal 1. the city where the government of a nation or state is located. Washington, D.C., is the capital of the United States. **2.** A, B, C, or any large letter. **cap i tals.**

car a vehicle, such as an automobile, that can carry people and baggage. **cars.**

cas tle a large building with thick walls and towers. **cas tles.**

cat a small animal often kept as a pet. **cats.**

catch 1. take and hold something that is moving: *Try to catch the ball in the air.* **2.** the act of catching: *She made a good catch in the ball game.* **caught, catch ing; catch es.**

one **cent**

caught See **catch.** *He caught more fish.*

cel e bra tion special activities in honor of a person or a day: *a birthday celebration.* **cel e bra tions.**

cent a coin worth one cent; a penny. One hundred cents are equal to one dollar. **cents.**

change 1. make different: *She changed the color of the wall from white to blue.* **2.** put something in place of another: *Please change your shoes.* **3.** a changing: *There was a change in our plans.* **4.** money you get back: *The clerk gave me five cents change.* **changed, chang ing, chang es.**

clock

check **1.** prove true or right by comparing: *Check your answers with hers.* **2.** a mark (√); a mark to show that something has been checked. **3.** a written order for money from a bank account. **checked, check ing; checks.**

chew crush with the teeth. **chewed, chew ing.**

chick en **1.** a young hen or rooster: *A female chicken lays eggs.* **2.** meat from a chicken. **chick ens.**

child a young boy or girl: *Where is that child?* **chil dren.**

chil dren more than one young boy or girl.

chin the part of your face below the mouth. **chins.**

chop **1.** cut by hitting with something sharp: *The man chopped down a tree with an ax.* **2.** cut into small pieces: *The cook chopped an onion.* **chopped, chop ping.**

clap **1.** a sudden noise like thunder or the sound of hands struck together. **2.** make such a noise with the hands: *They all clapped after the band played.* **claps; clapped, clap ping.**

class **1.** a group of persons or things of the same kind. **2.** a group of pupils taught together. **class es.**

climb go up something too steep to walk up: *I climbed a tree.* **climbed, climb ing.**

clock an instrument for measuring time. **clocks.**

clothes coverings for the body: *Dresses, pants, and shirts are clothes.*

club **1.** a heavy stick of wood. **2.** a stick or bat used to hit a ball in some games. **3.** a group of people joined together: *Kim belongs to the ski club.* **clubs.**

coach **1.** a vehicle pulled by horses, used to carry passengers before railroads were built. **2.** a person who teaches or trains people. **3.** train or teach. **coach es; coached, coach ing.**

coin a piece of metal used as money, such as a penny, a nickel, a dime or a quarter. **coins.**

come **1.** move toward: *Come over to me.* **2.** get near or to a place: *Will the girls come to your house?* **3.** take place; happen: *Winter has not come yet.* **came, come, com ing.**

com mu ni ty a group of people living together. A neighborhood or a town or a nation can be a community. **com mu ni ties.**

com pare find out or point out how persons or things are alike or different: *The girls compared their new red coats.* **com pared, com par ing.**

con cert a performance in which musicians play or sing. **con certs.**

cook ie a small, flat, sweet cake. **cook ies.**

cool **1.** more cold than hot: *a cool day.* **2.** giving a cool feeling: *a cool dress.* **cool er, cool est.**

cos tume clothes; what a person is wearing: *In our play I wore a king's costume.* **cos tumes.**

cou gar a large wildcat found in North and South America. **cou gars.**

could was able; was able to: *She wouldn't sew even if she could. She could swim.*

count **1.** name numbers in order: *He can count to one hundred.* **2.** add up: *He counted the pennies.* **count ed, count ing.**

football **coach** and player

cougar

course 1. the direction taken: *Our course was east.* **2. Of course** means certainly. **3.** one of the classes taken in school. **cours es.**

cous in the son or daughter of your uncle or aunt. **cous ins.**

crab a water animal, used for food. **crabs.**

crawl 1. creep; move slowly, pulling the body along: *We watched a caterpillar crawl along the leaf.* **2.** move slowly on hands and knees: *The boy crawled through the tall grass.* **crawled, crawl ing.**

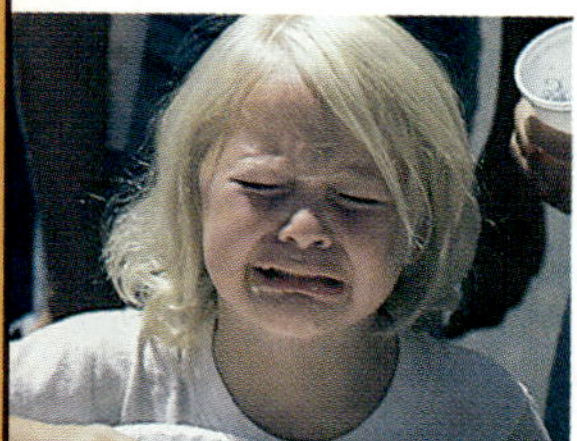

The girl is **crying.**

creek a small stream of water; a brook. **creeks.**

creep move slowly with the body close to the ground or floor; crawl. **crept, creep ing.**

cry 1. call loudly: *She cried, "Look out!"* **2.** make a noise, usually with tears: *Babies cry.* **cries, cried, cry ing.**

cup 1. a dish to drink from, usually with high sides and a handle. **2.** something shaped like a cup. **cups.**

cut 1. separate or take away with something sharp: *Cut the grass.* **2.** make by cutting: *He cut a hole through the paper.* **3.** a hole made by a knife or sharp tool. **cut, cut ting; cuts.**

D d

dandelion

dad another word for father. **dads.**

dan de li on a weed with bright-yellow flowers. **dan de li ons.**

dan ger ous able to cause harm; not safe.

daugh ter a girl who is the child of her father and mother: *Mr. and Mrs. Jones have three daughters.* **daugh ters.**

day **1.** the time of light between sunrise and sunset: *Days are getting shorter in November.* **2.** one of the seven 24 hour time periods that make up a week. **days.**

day time the time of day when it is light; time when it is day and not night.

desk a piece of furniture with a slanting or flat top on which to write. **desks.**

de tec tive a person whose business is to get facts and solve mysteries. **de tec tives.**

dia mond **1.** a stone of great value. **2.** a figure shaped like this (◇). **3.** part of a baseball field. **dia monds.**

dic tion ar y a book in which words are listed alphabetically. A dictionary tells what words mean. **dic tion ar ies.**

did See **do.** *Did he see them yesterday?*

dif fer ent not alike; separate: *These flowers are all different.*

dig **1.** make a hole in or turn over the ground: *Dig a ditch.* **2.** make or get by digging: *Dig clams.* **dug, dig ging.**

di rec tion **1.** the control of; the act of directing: *The school play is under the direction of our teacher.* **2.** the act of telling where to go or how to do: *Can you give me directions to the park? Follow the directions on the box.* **3.** any way in which one may face or point. North, south, east, and west are directions. **di rec tions.**

dish **1.** a container for food. **2.** food served: *My favorite dish is pie.* **dish es.**

do **1.** carry out an action or a piece of work: *Try to do your work.* **2.** act; behave: *We do well in school.* **does, did, done, do ing.**

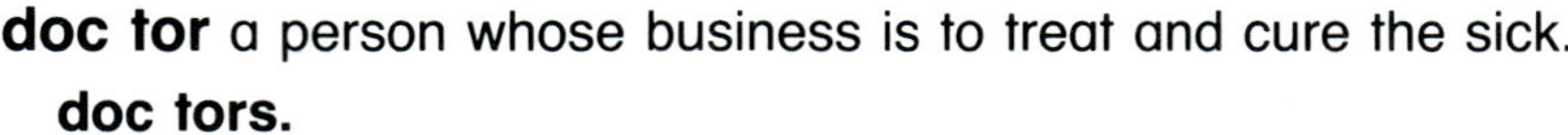

doc tor a person whose business is to treat and cure the sick. **doc tors.**

dog an animal used as a pet, for hunting, and for guarding property. **dogs.**

dog pad dle a form of swimming in which the arms paddle and the legs kick.

dog

doll a toy that looks like a person. **dolls.**

don't do not.

drag pull or move along the ground: *She dragged the big old box.* **dragged, drag ging.**

drag on in stories, a creature like a huge snake that breathes fire. **drag ons.**

draw 1. pull; get or take out: *Draw money from the bank.* **2.** make a picture of anything with pen, pencil, or chalk. **draws, drew, drawn, draw ing.**

dress 1. a piece of clothing worn by women and girls. **2.** put clothes on: *He can dress himself.* **dress es; dressed, dress ing.**

three **ducks**

duck[1] a swimming bird with a flat bill. **ducks.**

duck[2] **1.** dip the head or body under water and come up quickly, as a duck does. **2.** bend the body quickly to keep off a blow. **ducked, duck ing.**

E e

each all of a group but thought of one by one: *Each boy in the class has his lunch.*

earth quake a shaking of the ground, caused by the movement of rock far under the surface of the earth. **earth quakes.**

easy **1.** not hard to do or understand: *This was an easy lesson.* **2.** free from pain or trouble: *Climb this hill the easy way.* **eas i er, eas i est.**

eat chew and swallow food or have a meal. **ate, eat en, eat ing.**

egg **1.** the object laid by female birds, fish, and reptiles. Their young are hatched from eggs. **2.** the contents of an egg, used as food: *She eats two boiled eggs every morning.* **eggs.**

a dozen **eggs**

eight one more than seven; 8. **eights.**

eighth **1.** next after the seventh; 8th. **2.** one of 8 equal parts. **eighths.**

end **1.** the last part; the part where a thing begins or where it stops. **2.** finish something: *Let's end this fight right now.* **ends; end ed, end ing.**

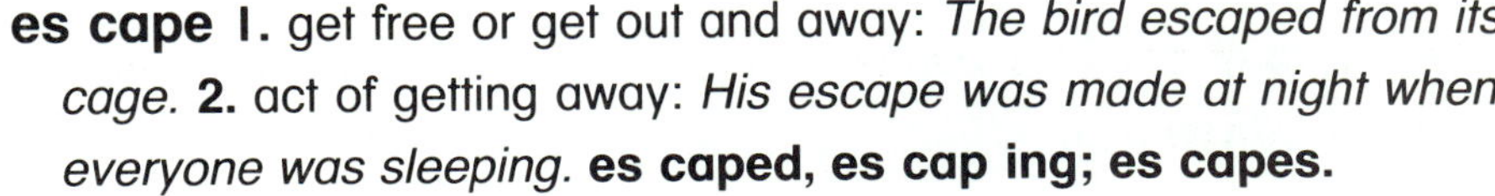

es cape **1.** get free or get out and away: *The bird escaped from its cage.* **2.** act of getting away: *His escape was made at night when everyone was sleeping.* **es caped, es cap ing; es capes.**

eve ry one each one; everybody.

eye **1.** the part of the body by which you see. **2.** something like an eye: *the eye of a needle.* **eyes.**

F f

fall **1.** come down from a higher place: *Leaves are falling.* **2.** the coming down from a higher place: *She had a bad fall down the stairs.* **3.** the part of the year after summer and before winter; autumn. **fell, fall en, fall ing; falls.**

fam i ly **1.** a parent or parents and a child or children. **2.** all of a person's relatives: *Grandmother invited the whole family.* **fam i lies.**

far a long way; a long way off: *Is it far to the store? The moon is far away.* **far ther, far thest.**

farm yard the yard around the farm buildings. **farm yards.**

field 1.

fa ther a male parent. **fa thers.**

feel **1.** touch: *Feel the smooth stone.* **2.** be; have in the mind: *She feels sad. I have felt sad too.* **felt, feel ing.**

feet more than one foot: *A person has two feet. Bill is four feet tall.*

few **1.** not many: *There are a few pieces of cake left.* **2.** a small number: *There are only a few people in the room.* **few er, few est.**

field **1.** land used for crops or for pasture. **2.** land for a special use: *a baseball field.* **fields.**

firefighter

fifth **1.** next after the fourth; 5th. **2.** one of 5 equal parts. **fifths.**

find **1.** come upon: *She found a dime.* **2.** look for and get: *Did you find your other shoe?* **found, find ing.**

fine **1.** very small or thin: *She drew a fine line with her pen. Sugar is ground fine.* **2.** excellent; very good: *He cooked a fine meal.* **fin er, fin est.**

fire fight er a person whose work is putting out fires. **fire fight ers.**

first **1.** coming before all others: *He is first in line.* **2.** before anything else: *We ate first and then played ball.* **3.** what is first; the beginning: *At first, I did not like him.*

fish 1. an animal that lives and breathes in water and has fins but no legs. **2.** catch fish; try to catch fish: *We fished with worms.* **fish es** or **fish; fished, fish ing.**

five one more than four: 5. *Five and five make ten.* **fives.**

flag a piece of colored cloth that stands for some country or state or group. **flags.**

flag pole pole from which a flag is flown. **flag poles.**

flat smooth and level: even; *We spread out our lunch on a flat rock.* **flat ter, flat test.**

flew See **fly²**. *The butterfly flew away. My dad flew in an airplane to Alaska.*

flow er the part of a plant or tree, often beautiful in color and shape, that bears the seed. **flow ers.**

fly¹ an insect with two wings. **flies.**

fly² 1. move through the air with wings: *Birds fly.* **2.** float in the air: *Our flag flies every day we are in school.* **3.** cause to fly: *The boys are flying model airplanes.* **4.** go through the air in an airplane. **flew, flown, fly ing.**

fog a cloud of fine drops of water just above the ground, thick and white, sometimes impossible to see through. **fogs.**

folk tale an old story that has been told for many years by many people. **folk tales.**

food anything that plants, animals, or people eat or drink that makes them live and grow. **foods.**

foot 1. the end part of a leg; the part that you stand on. **2.** a measure of length. Twelve inches are equal to one foot. **feet.**

fish 1.

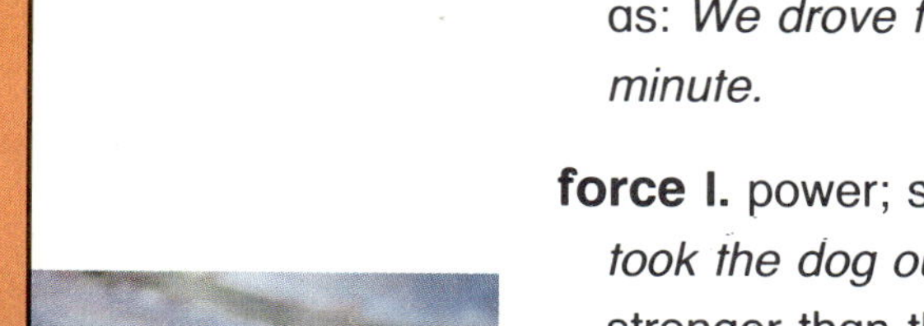

for **1.** in place of: *He gave me a dime for two nickels.* **2.** with the idea of: *He lay down for a nap.* **3.** meant to be used with: *a bank for pennies.* **4.** because of: *A party was given for her.* **5.** as far as: *We drove for twenty miles.* **6.** as long as: *We talked for a minute.*

force **1.** power; strength. **2.** power used against someone: *They took the dog out of the car by force.* **3.** get or take by being stronger than the thing or person against you. **forc es; forced, forc ing.**

fox

four one more than three; 4: *Four and four make eight.* **fours.**

fourth **1.** next after the third; 4th. **2.** a quarter; one of 4 equal parts. **fourths.**

fox a small, sly, wild animal. **fox es.**

free **1.** loose; not fastened or shut up. **2.** not under another person's control. **3.** not held back from acting or thinking as one pleases: *She was free to say what she thought.* **4.** without paying: *free tickets. We got in free.* **fre er, fre est.**

frog

friend a person who knows and likes you. **friends.**

frog a small, leaping animal that lives near water. **frogs.**

from **1.** out of: *Steel is made from iron.* **2.** beginning with: *Two weeks from today school is over.* **3.** because of: *She is suffering from mosquito bites.* **4.** off of: *He took a piece of fruit from the plate.*

fun a good time; amusement: *We had fun at the party.*

fun ny **1.** causing laughter: *The clown's funny actions kept us laughing.* **2.** foolish; silly. **fun ni er, fun ni est.**

G g

game something to play or a contest with certain rules: *This store sells games.* **games.**

gave See **give.** *He gave me a cookie.*

get **1.** be given; come to have: *I hope to get a bike for my birthday.* **2.** cause to be or do: *Can you get the window open?* **3.** become: *It gets hot in the summer.* **got, got** or **got ten, get ting.**

gi raffe a large animal with a very long neck. Giraffes are the tallest living animals. **gi raffes.**

girl a female child. **girls.**

give **1.** hand over as a present or gift. **2.** pay: *I will give you three dollars for the necklace.* **3.** do or make: *The dog gave me a scare when it barked.* **gave, giv en, giv ing.**

glove a covering for the hand, with a place for each finger and for the thumb. **gloves.**

go **1.** move along: *Boats go down the river.* **2.** move away: *Are you ready to go?* **3.** have its place; belong: *This dish goes on the first shelf.* **goes, went, gone, go ing.**

goat an animal with horns, a beard, and hoofs. **goats.**

gone See **go.** *She has gone home.*

good **1.** as it should be or well done: *She does good work.* **2.** doing what is right. **3.** pleasant: *I hope you have a good time at the ball game.* **4.** pleasant to the taste: *My birthday cake was very good.*

two **goats**

goose a bird that looks like a duck but is larger. It has webbed feet. **geese.**

got See **get.** *It got chilly.*

grab take suddenly or snatch: *The dog grabbed my shoe and ran.* **grabbed, grab bing.**

grand fa ther the father of one's father or mother. **grand fa thers.**

green 1. the color of most growing plants. **2.** having this color: *a green leaf, a green dress.* **3.** not ripe. **greens; green er, green est.**

grow 1. become bigger; become more. **2.** cause to grow; raise: *We grow corn on our farm.* **grew, grown, grow ing.**

guess 1. an idea you have that may not be right: *My guess is that the tree is ten feet high.* **2.** think without really knowing: *I guess it will rain tomorrow.* **guess es; guessed, guess ing.**

gum[1] something sweet that you chew but don't swallow.

gum[2] the part of the mouth around the teeth. **gums.**

H h

had See **have.** *We had a good time at the movie. I had a dime.*

half one of two equal parts: *Half of 6 is 3.* **halves.**

hand 1. the end part of the arm. **2.** something like a hand: *the hands of a clock.* **3.** give with the hand; pass: *Please hand me the salt.* **hands; hand ed, hand ing.**

hap py 1. feeling good; glad; pleased. **2.** showing that you are glad: *a happy smile.* **hap pi er, hap pi est.**

two **geese**

hard **1.** stiff; firm; not soft; not moving when touched: *Most nuts have hard shells.* **2.** needing much work or time: *This was a hard job to do.* **hard er, hard est.**

has See **have.** *Who has my boots?*

has n't has not.

have **1.** hold: *I have a snake in my hand.* **2.** own: *I have two dollars.* **3.** know; understand: *You have the right idea.* **4.** be forced: *I have to leave now.* **has, had, hav ing.**

have n't have not.

he any boy, man, or male animal you are talking about: *Joe says he goes to work every day. He is strong.*

health **1.** being well or not being sick. **2. Health,** a school subject that teaches the proper care of the body.

hear **1.** get sounds through the ear: *Can you hear my watch?* **2.** receive word or news: *Did you hear from your sister?* **heard, hear ing.**

heat **1.** extreme warmth: *The heat of a stove feels good on a cold day.* **2.** make or become warm, or hot: *The furnace heats the house.* **heat ed, heat ing.**

hel i cop ter aircraft without wings that is lifted from the ground and kept in the air by one or more propellers. **hel i cop ters.**

helicopter

hen a female chicken or other female bird. **hens.**

her **1.** any girl or woman or female animal you are talking about: *Sue is here; have you seen her? Wait for her.* **2.** of her; belonging to her; done by her: *Peg hurt her arm. It's her fault.*

here in this place; at this place: *Do you live here?*

hide **1.** put out of sight: *Hide the candy.* **2.** be in front of: *That picture hides a crack in the wall.* **3.** keep secret: *She tried to hide her fear.* **hid, hid den** or **hid, hid ing.**

high **1.** tall: *a high hill.* **2.** up above the ground: *a high step.* **3.** at or to a high place. **high er, high est.**

hill a raised part of the earth's surface, not so big as a mountain. **hills.**

skiing down a **hill**

him any boy or man or male animal you are talking about: *Did you thank him? She gave him money.*

his **1.** of him; belonging to him: *His bicycle is lost.* **2.** the one or ones belonging to him: *My shoes are black; his are brown.*

hold **1.** take or pick up and keep: *Hold this suitcase for me.* **2.** the act of holding: *I took a good hold of the knob and pulled.* **held, hold ing.**

hold 1.

hol i day a day when you do not work or go to school; a day for having fun: *The fourth of July is a holiday for everyone.* **hol i days.**

home **1.** the place where a person or a family lives. **2.** the town or country where you were born or brought up: *Her home town is San Francisco.* **homes.**

home work **1.** work done at home. **2.** lessons to be done at home.

hom o phone word that has the same sound as another, but a different meaning. *Ate* is a homophone of *eight. See* and *sea* are also homphones. **hom o phones.**

hop **1.** spring, or move by springing: *How far can you hop on one foot? The rabbit hopped across the field.* **2.** a spring: *Take two hops forward and one hop back.* **hopped, hop ping; hops.**

hope I. a feeling that what you want to happen will happen: *Her words gave me hope.* **2.** look for; expect: *I hope you'll like school.* **hopes; hoped, hop ing.**

hot I. having much heat: *Today was a very hot day. The vegetable soup was too hot to eat.* **2.** having a sharp, burning taste: *Dad cooked a very hot chili for dinner.* **hot ter, hot test.**

hour a period of time; one of the 24 equal parts of one day. Sixty minutes make an hour. **hours.**

hug I. put your arms around and hold close: *The little boy hugs his puppy.* **2.** a tight pressure with the arms: *When I come home, I expect a hug.* **hugged, hug ging; hugs.**

hurt I. do harm to: *The stones will hurt your feet.* **2.** suffer pain: *Your head hurt, didn't it? Has it hurt all day?* **hurt, hurt ing.**

I i

I the person speaking: *I am here. I am running.*

if I. not certain or sure: *I'll go to the park if it doesn't rain.* **2.** whether: *I wonder if I should go to the movie.*

I'll I. I shall. **2.** I will.

I'm I am.

in I. within; not outside: *We live in the city, but my grandparents live in the country.* **2.** during: *in the winter, in an hour.* **3.** into: *Go in the house.* **4.** *on the inside: Dad is working in the garage.*

inch a measure of length. There are twelve inches in one foot. **inch es.**

in side **I.** the part within; the surface not on the outside: *The inside of the box was covered with silk.* **2.** in: *He is inside the car.*

in to **I.** to the inside of: *The cows walked into the barn.* **2.** to the form of: *Heat turns ice into water.*

in ves ti gate search into; ask questions about: *The police investigated the crime.* **in ves ti gat ed, in ves ti gat ing.**

Their **job** is feeding seals

is *My head is cold. He is at home. She is going. It is hot inside.The house is heated with gas.*

is n't is not.

it the thing or animal spoken about: *Look at that bird; is it hurt? It looks like rain. My head hurts; I bumped it.*

it's **I.** it is: *It's going to rain.* **2.** it has: *It's rained all day.*

I've I have.

J j

jack et **I.** a short coat. **2.** an outside covering: *New books have paper jackets.* **jack ets.**

jump

job **I.** work; anything a person has to do: *It was Mark's job to pass out the crayons.* **2.** work done for pay: *My mom has a job in a store.* **jobs.**

jump **I.** leave the ground by pushing the body upward or off: *Jump over that rock.* **2.** a spring from the ground; a leap: *The horse made a high jump over the fence.* **jumped, jump ing; jumps.**

just **I.** truly; in fact. **2.** exactly: *The apples weighed just a pound.* **3.** a little while ago: *He just came back from vacation.* **4.** only: *He is just going to the corner.*

K k

keep **1.** have forever: *Grandmother said I could keep this ring.* **2.** have and not let go: *I know she can keep a secret.* **3.** hold back: *We kept the dog from running away.* **kept, keep ing.**

kick **1.** strike out with the foot: *The baby likes to kick his feet.* **2.** a blow with the foot. **kicked, kick ing; kicks.**

kick ball a game that is similar to baseball. The ball is rolled instead of thrown, and kicked instead of hit.

kid **1.** a young goat. **2.** a child. **kids.**

kind[1] friendly; doing good rather than harm: *a kind person.* **kind er, kind est.**

kind[2] a group of things that are alike. **kinds.**

kite a wooden frame covered with paper. Kites are flown in the air on the end of a long string. **kites.**

kit ten a young cat. **kit tens.**

knew See **know.** *I knew she'd come today.*

know **1.** tell apart from others: *How many kinds of cars do you know?* **2.** have as a friend: *Do you know my aunt?* **3.** have the facts about; be aware of. **knew, known, know ing.**

L l

la dy a woman. **la dies.**

land **1.** the solid part of the earth's surface. **2.** ground; soil: *Our farm has good land.* **3.** a country: *He came from a distant land.* **4.** come to shore. **lands; land ed, land ing.**

kite

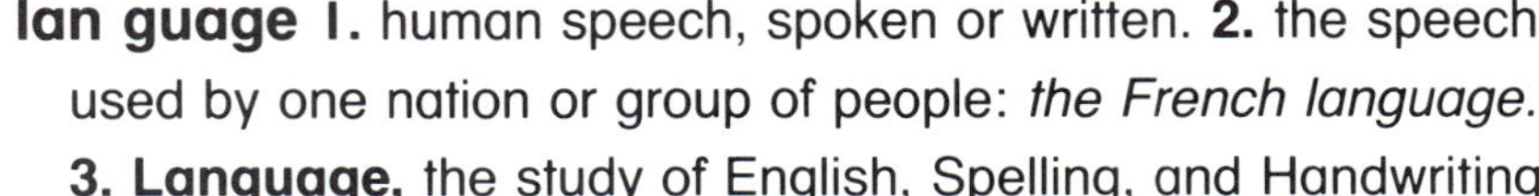

lan guage **1.** human speech, spoken or written. **2.** the speech used by one nation or group of people: *the French language.* **3. Language,** the study of English, Spelling, and Handwriting.

leaf one of the thin, flat, usually green parts of a plant. **leaves.**

leaf

let **1.** not stop someone or something from doing something: *She let the kitten play by itself.* **2.** allow something to happen. **let, let ting.**

light[1] **1.** that by which we see: *The sun gives light.* **2.** something that gives light: *Bring a light into this room.* **3.** give light to; fill with light: *Dad lighted the lamp with a match.* **lights; light ed** or **lit, light ing.**

light[2] easy to lift; not heavy. **light er, light est.**

like[1] the same as: *Sue is like her mother.*

like[2] be pleased with; be satisfied with: *Most children like to play games.* **liked, lik ing.**

li on a large, strong, wild animal. The lion is sometimes called the king of beasts. **lions.**

lion

lip either of the two edges of the mouth. **lips.**

lla ma a South American animal something like a camel, but smaller and without a hump. Llamas have woolly hair. **lla mas.**

lob ster a sea animal with two large claws. **lob sters.**

log **1.** a long piece from the trunk or branches of a tree. **2.** made of logs: *a log cabin.* **logs.**

long having great distance from end to end or from beginning to end: *An inch is short; a mile is long.* **long er, long est.**

look **1.** see; turn your eyes toward: *Look at me.* **2.** search; try to find: *Did you look in the closet for your cap?* **3.** the act of looking: *He gave me an angry look.* **looked, look ing; looks.**

lot **1.** a piece of land: *an empty lot.* **2.** a great many; very much: *a lot of fish, a lot of work.* **lots.**

lucky having or bringing good luck: *Three is my lucky number.* **luck i er, luck i est.**

lunch a light meal: *We usually have lunch at noon.* **lunch es.**

M m

made See **make.** *My sister made my birthday cake. She has made one every year.*

mail **1.** letters and parcels sent from one person to another by the post office department. **2.** send by mail: *Please mail this letter.* **mailed, mail ing.**

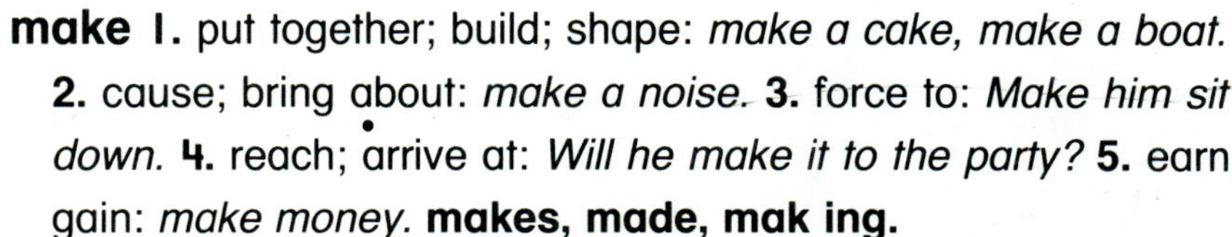

make **1.** put together; build; shape: *make a cake, make a boat.* **2.** cause; bring about: *make a noise.* **3.** force to: *Make him sit down.* **4.** reach; arrive at: *Will he make it to the party?* **5.** earn; gain: *make money.* **makes, made, mak ing.**

man a male human being. A man is a boy grown up. **men.**

ma ny a great number of: *Many years ago the house was new.* **more, most.**

map a drawing of the earth's surface or part of it. Some maps show countries, cities, rivers, oceans, lakes, and so on. **maps.**

mask a covering to hide or protect the face: *He wore a mask with his costume.* **masks.**

a firefighter's **mask**

math e mat ics **1.** science that deals with the study of numbers and measurement. Arithmetic is one part of mathematics. **2. Mathematics,** school subject that deals with the study of numbers and measurement.

may **1.** allow to: *You may have an apple.* **2.** be possible that it will: *Do you think it may rain tomorrow? Our flight may be late.* **might.**

milk 1.

me the person speaking: *Give me the dog.*

mean[1] **1.** have in mind; want to say: *What does that word mean?* **2.** plan to do: *You didn't mean to break the toy.* **meant, mean ing.**

mean[2] unkind; cruel: *It is mean to tease the puppy.* **mean er, mean est.**

mean ing what is meant: *Do you know the meaning of this word?* **mean ings.**

meet **1.** come face to face with: *I don't want to meet another car on this narrow road.* **2.** come together; join: *Two roads meet at the corner.* **3.** be introduced to: *I want you to meet my sister.* **met, meet ing.**

men more than one man: *Boys grow up to be men.*

met See **meet.** *They met in the park.*

milk **1.** the white liquid, from cows, which we drink and use in cooking. **2.** draw milk from a cow. **milked, milk ing.**

mil lion one thousand thousand; 1,000,000: *I wish I had a million dollars.* **mil lions.**

mind **1.** the part of a person that thinks: *She has a good mind.* **2.** take care of: *Please mind the baby.* **3.** pay attention. **minds; mind ed, mind ing.**

min ute **1.** one of sixty equal parts of an hour; sixty seconds. **2.** a short time: *We should be there in a minute.* **min utes.**

miss **1.** fail to hit: *He missed the ball when he swung.* **2.** fail to get: *Don't miss the train.* **3.** leave out or skip: *She missed a word when she read the sentence.* **4.** notice or feel bad because something is gone: *We miss you.* **missed, miss ing.**

mod el **1.** a copy, usually small: *a ship model.* **2.** make or shape: *Let's model an elephant.* **mod els; mod eled, mod el ing.**

mom mother. **moms.**

mon ey coins and paper bills used in buying and selling things.

month one of the twelve parts of a year. **months.**

moon a heavenly body that revolves around the earth. **moons.**

more **1.** larger in size or amount: *A pound is more than an ounce. This soup needs more salt.* **2.** a greater amount or number: *We need more than ten players for the team.*

morn ing the early part of the day, ending at noon. **morn ings.**

most **1.** greatest or largest in amount: *Ice-skating is the most fun of all.* **2.** the greatest amount or number. **3.** almost all: *Most people like music.*

moth er a female parent. **moth ers.**

mo tion the act of moving from one position to another: *The motion of the ship made him sick.* **mo tions.**

much a large amount of; a certain amount of: *much trouble, how much?* **more, most.**

mud wet earth that is soft and sticky.

moon

must be forced to: *You must eat the right food. I must go now.*

my of me; belonging to me: *I forgot my gloves.*

my self *Myself* is used instead of *me* in sentences such as: *I can do it myself. I cut myself.* **our selves.**

N n

name 1. the word or words by which a person, animal, place, or thing is spoken of or to: *His name is Jack.* **2.** give a name to: *They named the baby Helen after her aunt.* **names; named, nam ing.**

nap 1. a short sleep: *The baby takes a nap after lunch.* **2.** take a short sleep or rest: *Grandfather naps in his armchair.* **naps; napped, nap ping.**

neck 1. the part of the body between the head and shoulders. **2.** the part of a piece of clothing that fits the neck. **necks.**

need be in want of; ought to have; not be able to do without: *We need food.* **need ed, need ing.**

neigh bor hood 1. the streets and houses surrounding the place you live. **2.** of a neighborhood: *a neighborhood newspaper.* **neigh bor hoods.**

neigborhood 1.

new 1. never made or used before. **2.** not old or used up. **new er, new est.**

nick el 1. a metal that looks somewhat like silver. **2.** a United States or Canadian coin worth five cents. **nick els.**

night 1. the time between evening and morning. **2.** of or for night: *night wind, night light.* **3.** evening; nightfall. **nights.**

nine one more than eight: 9. *Nine and nine make eighteen.* **nines.**

ninth 1. next after the eighth; 9th. **2.** one of 9 equal parts. **ninths.**

no 1. a word used to say you can't or won't. **2.** not any: *Worms have no legs.* **noes.**

no bod y no one; no person. **no bod ies.**

nose the part of your face or head just above the mouth. **nos es.**

not a word that says "no": *Down is not up.*

noth ing no thing: *We could see nothing. Nothing happened.*

nu mer al a figure or group of figures standing for a number. 2, 5, 12, 117 are numerals. **nu mer als.**

nut 1. a dry fruit or seed. **2.** a small metal block with a hole in the center into which a screw fits. **nuts.**

ocean

O o

ob serve 1. see and notice: *Did you observe anything strange about her?* **2.** look at closely: *An astronomer observes the stars.*

o cean a great body of salt water. The oceans cover almost three fourths of the earth's surface. **o ceans.**

o'clock of the clock; by the clock: *Meet me at twelve o'clock.*

oc to pus a sea animal. It has a soft, thick body and eight arms. **oc to pus es.**

of 1. belonging to: *The members of the team went home.* **2.** made from: *They built a house of bricks.* **3.** named: *The state of Texas is very big.*

off **1.** from; away from: *The cat jumped off the bench.* **2.** away; at a distance: *He went off by himself.* **3.** not on; not connected: *The radio is off.*

old not young or new. **old er, old est.**

on **1.** upon: *The lizard is on the rock.* **2.** touching so as to cover or be around: *Put your left shoe on your left foot.*

once **1.** one time: *Play that song once more.* **2.** at some time in the past: *The plant was once a seed.*

one **1.** the number 1. **2.** a single: *one chair, one day.* **3.** a single thing: *Which one do you want? I want that one.* **ones.**

on ly **1.** by itself; one and no more: *an only child. This is the only road to town.* **2.** just: *She had three papers but she sold only two.* **3.** alone: *She was the one and only child.*

or *Or* is used when there is something to choose: *Is it hot or cold? She didn't know whether to laugh or cry.*

or ange **1.** a round, yellowish-red fruit, full of juice, that is good to eat. **2.** the tree it grows on. **3.** the color of an orange. **or ang es.**

or bit **1.** the path of a planet around the sun; the path of a satellite around the earth. **2.** travel around the earth or some other body in an orbit: *The satellite began to orbit at 6:02 a.m.* **or bits; or bit ed, or bit ing.**

os trich a large, long-legged bird that can run fast but cannot fly. **os trich es.**

o ver **1.** above: *the roof over our heads.* **2.** on or to the other side of; across: *The stream was so narrow we could jump over it.* **3.** at an end; finished: *The movie is over.* **4.** more than: *It costs over ten dollars.*

orange 1.

own 1. have; keep because you bought it or because someone gave it to you: *I own a football.* **2.** belonging to oneself or itself: *I make my own bed.* **owned, own ing.**

P p

paint 1. a thick liquid that you put on a surface to color and protect it. **2.** cover with paint. **3.** draw a picture in colors: *The artist will paint a picture.* **paints; paint ed, paint ing.**

parrot

pa rade 1. a march or a walk for some special event: *Clowns were in the circus parade.* **2.** march or walk for some special event. **pa rades; pa rad ed, pa rad ing.**

par ent a person's father or mother. **par ents.**

par rot a brightly colored bird. It can be taught to say words. **par rots.**

part 1. less than the whole; not all: *He ate only part of his dinner.* **2.** a thing that helps make up something: *A string is one part of a guitar.* **3.** a line you make when you comb your hair. **parts; part ed, part ing.**

par ty 1. a group of people having a good time or doing something together: *a birthday party; a search party.* **2.** of or for a party: *a party dress.* **par ties.**

pass 1. go by; move beyond: *The truck passed two cars.* **2.** hand from one to another: *Please pass the meat.* **3.** succeed in a test: *She passed arithmetic.* **passed, pass ing.**

pat tap gently with the hand: *He patted the dog.* **pat ted, pat ting.**

peas ant a farmer of the working class in Europe. **peas ants.**

peek look quickly and slyly: *Close your eyes and do not peek.* **peeked, peek ing.**

pen[1] a tool used in writing with ink. **pens.**

pen[2] a small, closed place to keep babies or animals: *We put the pig in the pen.* **pens.**

pen[2]

pen ny a cent; a copper coin of the United States and Canada. Ten pennies make one dime. **pen nies.**

peo ple men, women, and children; persons: *There were only three people at the meeting.*

pe ri od 1. a length of time. **2.** a dot (.) marking the end of most sentences or of an abbreviation. **pe ri ods.**

pet 1. a favorite animal kept and treated with love. **2.** pat gently: *Pet the kitten.* **3.** treated as a pet: a *pet rabbit.* **pets; pet ted, pet ting.**

a boy and his **pet**

pet al one of the parts of a flower that are usually colored. A rose has many petals. **pet als.**

pick 1. choose: *I picked the brown shoes.* **2.** pull away with the fingers: *We pick flowers.* **picked, pick ing.**

pic nic a party with a meal outdoors. **pic nics.**

pig a hog; an animal raised for its meat. **pigs.**

pi lot 1. a person whose business is to steer a ship or an airplane. **2.** act as a pilot of; steer: *She piloted the ship up the river.* **pi lots; pi lot ed, pi lot ing.**

pin 1. a short, thin piece of wire with one sharp end to stick through things and fasten them together. **2.** fasten with a pin: *Pin the flower on her dress.* **pins; pinned, pin ning.**

pi rate a person who robs ships at sea. **pi rates.**

plain **1.** clear; easy to understand; easily seen or heard: *The meaning of this sentence is plain.* **2.** without any trimming: *He wore a plain shirt.* **plain er, plain est.**

plan **1.** something you have thought out to do: *Have you a plan for earning money?* **2.** think out how something is to be made or done: *We are planning the party.* **plans; planned, plan ning.**

plant **1.** any living thing that is not an animal. **2.** any living thing with leaves, roots, and a soft stem that is smaller than a tree or bush. **3.** put in the ground to grow: *Plant these seeds in the spring.* **plants; plant ed, plant ing.**

play **1.** fun; something done to amuse yourself: *There will be time for play after school.* **2.** have fun; do something in a sport: *Let's play ball.* **3.** a story acted on the stage: *We saw a play about pirates.* **plays; played, play ing.**

please **1.** give pleasure to: *Reading aloud to children pleases them.* **2.** be happy or delighted: *Sam was pleased with the flowers.* **3.** *Please* is a polite way of asking something. **pleased, pleas ing.**

po et ry poems.

po ta to a plant. Part of it grows under the ground and is eaten as a vegetable. **po ta toes.**

pret ty pleasing; sweet; charming; cute: *She wore a pretty coat.* **pret ti er, pret ti est.**

prince the son of a king or queen. **princ es.**

prin cess **1.** the daughter of a king or queen. **2.** the wife of a prince. **prin cess es.**

children **playing**

print er a person whose work is printing books, newspapers, magazines, and so on. **print ers.**

pup py a young dog. **pup pies.**

pur ple a dark color made by mixing red and blue. **pur ples.**

Q q

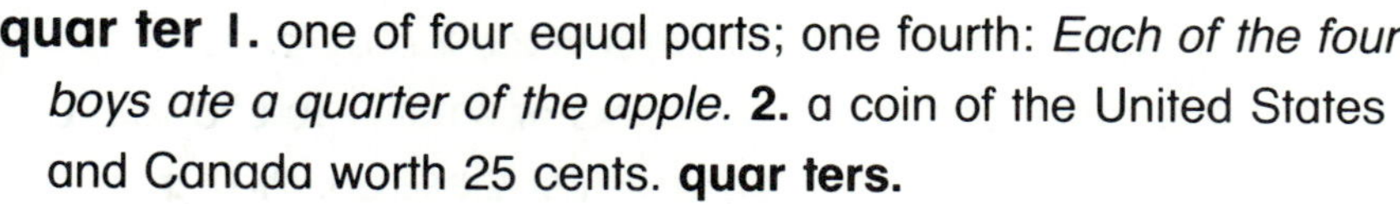

quar ter 1. one of four equal parts; one fourth: *Each of the four boys ate a quarter of the apple.* **2.** a coin of the United States and Canada worth 25 cents. **quar ters.**

rain **1.**

ques tion a thing asked to find out something: *A teacher asks questions.* **ques tions.**

quick sand soft, wet sand that people and animals sink into when they stand on it.

R r

rab bit an animal with soft fur and long ears. **rab bits.**

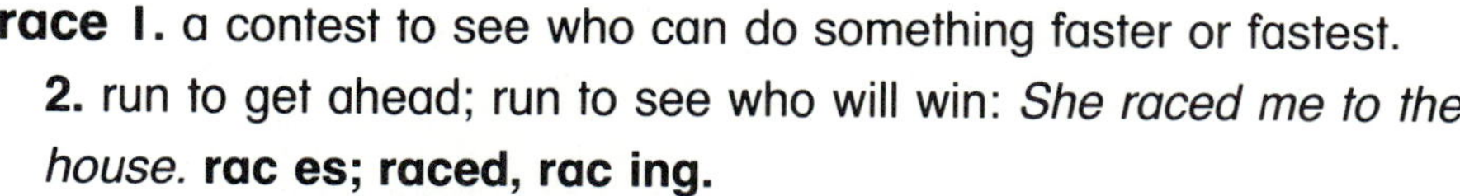

race 1. a contest to see who can do something faster or fastest. **2.** run to get ahead; run to see who will win: *She raced me to the house.* **rac es; raced, rac ing.**

a girl **reading**

rain 1. water falling in drops from the clouds: *The rain lasted all night.* **2.** fall in drops: *It rained all night.* **rains; rained, rain ing.**

ran See **run.** *She ran home.*

read[1] **1.** understand what writing or print means: *Have you learned to read?* **2.** speak out loud the words of writing or print: *Read this story.* **read, read ing.** (Read[1] rhymes with seed.)

read[2] See **read**[1]. *She read that book in school. Have you read it? (Read[2] rhymes with head.)*

red **1.** the color of blood. **2.** having that color. **reds; red der, red dest.**

ride **1.** sit on something and make it go: *Some people ride camels.* **2.** a trip on an animal or a vehicle: *We took a ride on our bikes.* **rode, rid den, rid ing; rides.**

right **1.** good; just: *The right thing to do is tell the truth.* **2.** something that a person should have or should be allowed to do: *Each citizen has a right to vote.* **3.** correct; true: *the right answer.* **4.** correctly; truly: *I guessed right.* **5.** opposite of left: *the right hand. Make a right turn.* **rights.**

robin

riv er a large stream of running water. **riv ers.**

rob in a large American bird with a reddish breast. **rob ins.**

rock **1.** the large masses of hard material found in the earth. **2.** a large stone. **rocks.**

rode See **ride.** *I rode my bicycle to school.*

room a part of a house or building: *I like to keep my room clean.* **rooms.**

rub move one thing back and forth against another. **rubbed, rub bing.**

rug a heavy floor covering: *Mom bought a new rug for my room.* **rugs.**

run **1.** go faster than walking: *Have you ever run a mile?* **2.** go in a hurry: *Run to the store.* **3.** go; move; work: *Why won't my watch run?* **runs, ran, run ning.**

S s

said See **say.** *He said it was true. He has said so.*

sand wich slices of bread with meat, jelly, or some other food between them. **sand wich es.**

sat See **sit.** *She sat down for a minute to rest. Grandmother has sat by the window all day.*

They **sat** on a log.

saw[1] **1.** a tool for cutting. **2.** cut with a saw: *Dad sawed the board in two.* **saws; sawed, sawed** or **sawn, saw ing.**

saw[2] See **see.** *I saw a bluebird in that tree.*

say speak; put into words. **said, say ing.**

scare crow a figure of a person dressed in old clothes. A scarecrow is set up in a field to frighten birds away. **scare crows.**

scarecrow

scarf a piece of cloth worn on the head or around the neck and shoulders. **scarves.**

scarves more than one scarf.

school[1] **1.** a place for teaching and learning: *My uncle goes to night school.* **2.** the pupils and teachers of a school: *Our whole school visited the zoo.* **schools.**

school[2] a large number of the same kind of fish or water animals swimming together: *a school of mackerel.* **schools.**

sci ence 1. a careful study of facts about the earth and about the plants and animals on it. Science also studies stars, planets, and space. **2. Science,** school subject that deals with a study of facts about the earth, plants, animals, stars, planets, and space. **sci enc es.**

search **1.** try to find by looking: *We searched everywhere for that book.* **2.** go over carefully: *The police searched the house.* **3.** the act of searching: *Everybody joined in the search for eggs.* **searched, search ing; search es.**

seat **1.** something to sit on. **2.** a place to sit: *Our seats are in the first row.* **3.** the part of a chair you sit on: *Put a cushion on the seat of that chair.* **4.** put into a seat: *He seated himself in the chair. I was seated next to the president.* **seats; seat ed, seat ing.**

sec ond next after the first; 2nd. *She won second prize at the art show.*

se cret **1.** something that you don't tell anyone. **2.** something not known to everyone. **se crets.**

see **1.** look at: *See the falling star!* **2.** find out: *Let's see what's wrong.* **3.** visit: *We went to see Grandmother.* **saw, seen, see ing.**

seem give the feeling of being: *The baby seemed hungry, but she wouldn't eat. The cat seems to like that toy. Does this radio seem too loud to you?* **seemed, seem ing.**

sell trade a thing for money: *I am going to sell my bike.* **sold, sell ing.**

send cause to go: *Mother often sends Frank to the store.* **sent, send ing.**

sent See **send.** *He sent us to look for water. Two of the children have been sent to the library.*

sen tence a group of words that is complete in itself. A sentence usually ends with a period or a question mark. **sen tenc es.**

searching for a book

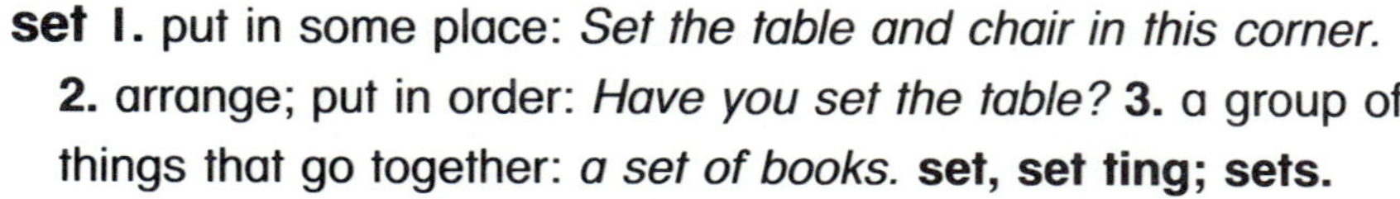

set **1.** put in some place: *Set the table and chair in this corner.* **2.** arrange; put in order: *Have you set the table?* **3.** a group of things that go together: *a set of books.* **set, set ting; sets.**

se ven one more than six; 7. **sev ens.**

sev enth **1.** next after the sixth; 7th. **2.** one of 7 equal parts. **sev enths.**

shell **1.**

shall *Shall* is used when something will happen or must happen: *I shall be there soon. You shall go to bed right now.* **should.**

she any girl, woman, or female animal spoken about before: *My sister says she will hurry home. She has many books.*

shell **1.** the hard covering of some animals. Snails, oysters, crabs, turtles, have shells. **2.** the hard covering of a nut or egg. **shells.**

ship **1.** a large boat. **2.** send or carry by ship, train, truck, or plane: *Will you ship the package to me?* **ships; shipped, ship ping.**

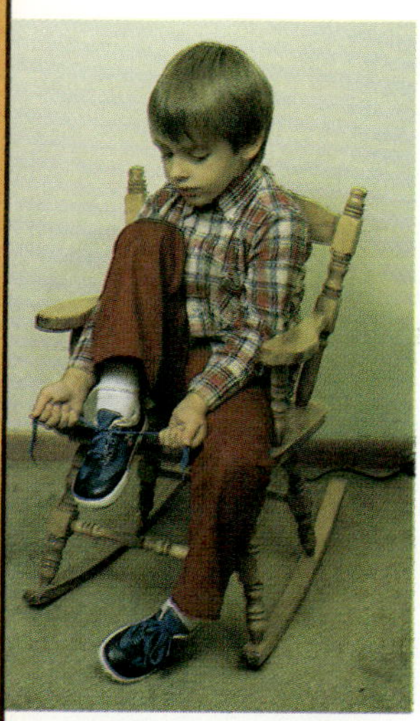

tying **shoelaces**

shoe lace a cord or string for fastening a shoe. **shoe lac es.**

shop **1.** a place where things are sold; a store. **2.** visit stores to buy things: *We shopped all day.* **shops; shopped, shop ping.**

short **1.** not tall: *The short children sit in the front seats.* **2.** not long: *Summer seems short.* **short er, short est.**

should **1.** *Should* is used to mean ought to: *She should be here by now. We should have known better.* **2.** *Should* can mean something may or may not happen: *If it should rain, we won't go.*

show **1.** bring or put in sight: *My aunt showed us her new car.* **2.** make clear to: *The salesperson showed me how to do the puzzle.* **3.** a play, movie, TV program: *We saw a good show.* **showed, shown** or **showed, show ing.**

sick not well; having a disease: *Is he sick?* **sick er, sick est.**

sil ly without good sense; without making any sense: *Those kids are acting silly. This is a silly joke.* **sil li er, sil li est.**

sil ver a shiny white metal of great value. Silver is used to make coins, jewelry, and tableware.

sing 1. make music with the voice: *He sings well.* **2.** make pleasant sounds: *Meadowlarks sing.* **sang** or **sung, sung, sing ing.**

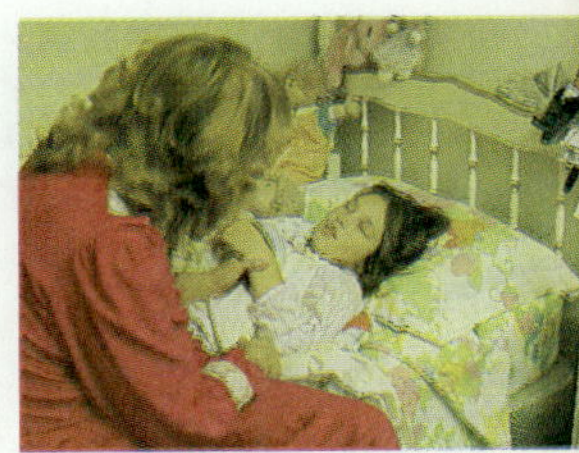

a **sick** child

sing er one who sings. **sing ers.**

sis ter a girl with the same parents as another. **sis ters.**

sit 1. rest on the lower part of the body. **2.** be placed: *The clock should sit on top of that corner cupboard.* **sat, sit ting.**

six one more than five; 6. **six es.**

sixth 1. next after the fifth; 6th. **2.** one of 6 equal parts. **sixths.**

sky space high above, that seems to cover the earth; the air above us. **skies.**

sled 1. framework of boards mounted on runners for use on snow or ice. **2.** ride or coast on a sled. **sleds; sled ded, sled ding.**

sleep rest your body and mind: *It's easy to sleep when it's quiet.* **slept, sleep ing.**

slow 1. taking a long time; not fast or quick: *a slow trip, a slow driver.* **2.** showing time earlier than the correct time: *I was late because the clock was slow.* **slow er, slow est.**

small 1. not large: *a small dog.* **2.** not much: *I ate a small amount of spinach.* **small er, small est.**

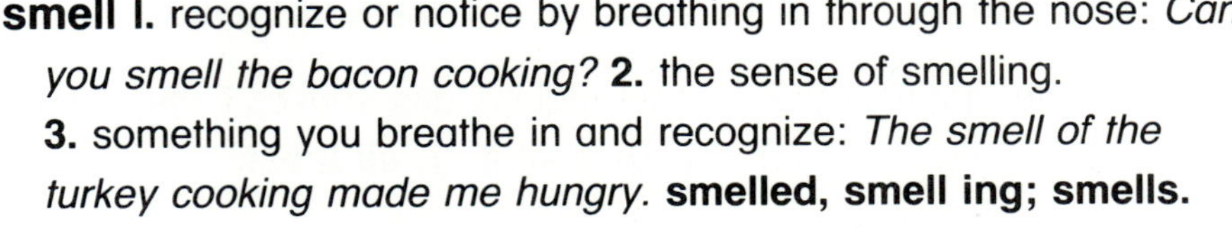

smell 1. recognize or notice by breathing in through the nose: *Can you smell the bacon cooking?* **2.** the sense of smelling. **3.** something you breathe in and recognize: *The smell of the turkey cooking made me hungry.* **smelled, smell ing; smells.**

smile 1. look happy by turning up the corners of your mouth: *The baby smiled.* **2.** the act of curving up the corners of the mouth to show you are pleased: *He has a nice smile.* **smiled, smil ing; smiles.**

a happy **smile**

so 1. in that way: *Don't eat so fast.* **2.** of such a size: *The fire was so big the firemen couldn't put it out.* **3.** for this reason: *The wind felt cold, so we went in.* **4.** very: *This tastes so good.*

social studies 1. the study of history, geography, government, and other such subjects. **2. Social Studies,** school subject that deals with the study of history, geography, government, and other such subjects.

sock a short knitted covering for the foot and leg. **socks.**

a pair of **socks**

soft ball 1. a kind of baseball game. A larger ball and lighter bats are used in softball than in baseball. **2.** ball used in this game. **soft balls.**

sol dier one who serves in an army. **sol diers.**

some 1. not all: *Some people like to swim; some don't* **2.** an amount of: *Drink some more water.*

some thing something; a certain thing not named or known: *I'm sure I've forgotten something.*

some times now and then; at times: *They come to visit sometimes.*

soon in a short time; before long: *Will I see you soon?* **soon er, soon est.**

spe cial of a kind different from all others: *a special day.*

sport a kind of game or amusement. Baseball is an outdoor sport. **sports.**

spot 1. a mark: *She has an ink spot on her sleeve.* **2.** a part different from the rest: *Peter's necktie is red with white spots.* **3.** a place: *From this spot on the hill you can see the valley.*

stamp 1. a small piece of paper with glue on the back. **2.** put a stamp on. **3.** bring down your foot with force. **4.** put a mark on: *Stamp this bill "Paid."* **stamps; stamped, stamp ing.**

star fish a sea animal shaped like a star. **star fish es** or **star fish.**

start 1. make the first move to do something or go somewhere: *The car started to roll.* **2.** the first move to do or go: *an early start.* **3.** a beginning. **start ed, start ing; starts.**

state ment something spoken or written that tells or explains a fact or idea: *She wrote a clear statement.* **state ments.**

stay continue to be in a place: *Stay in this chair.* **stayed, stay ing.**

stem 1. the main part of a plant above the ground. The stem of a tree is its trunk. **2.** the part of a flower, fruit, or leaf that joins it to the plant. **stems.**

step 1. a motion made by lifting the foot and putting it down in a new position: *Take three steps.* **2.** move the legs as in walking: *Step to the front of the line.* **3.** a place for the foot in going up or down: *cellar steps.* **steps; stepped, step ping.**

stew 1. cook by slow boiling. **2.** food cooked by slow boiling: *Betty made lamb stew.* **stewed, stew ing; stews.**

starfish

stir 1. move: *The breeze hardly stirs the leaves.* **2.** move about: *Everyone began to stir in the morning.* **3.** mix by moving around: *Stir the soup.* **stirred, stir ring.**

stone 1. hard material of the earth; rock. **stones.**

stop 1. keep from moving, working, doing, or being: *The red light stopped traffic.* **2.** come to an end. **stopped, stop ping.**

store 1. a place where things are kept for sale. **2.** put away for use later: *She stored her winter coat.* **stores; stored, stor ing.**

sto ry[1] an account, true or make-believe, of some things that have happened: *I hope he tells us the story of his life.* **sto ries.**

sto ry[2] the set of rooms on the same level or floor of a building: *My dollhouse has two stories.* **sto ries.**

stones

sum 1. all or a certain number of things put together: *I saved the sum of ten dollars.* **2.** two or more numbers or things added together: *The sum of 3 and 4 is 7.* **3.** the whole amount. **sums.**

stop 1.

sun 1. the star around which the earth revolves. It supplies heat and light. **2.** the light and heat of the sun: *I sat in the sun.* **suns.**

sun shine the shining of the sun; the light of the sun.

sur prise 1. something not expected: *The news was a surprise.* **2.** cause surprise: *He surprised us when he laughed.* **3.** coming as a surprise. **sur pris es; sur prised, sur pris ing.**

swam See **swim.** *Most of us swam a mile.*

swell grow bigger; make bigger: *Rain swelled the river.* **swelled, swelled** or **swol len, swell ing.**

swim

swim 1. move in water by moving fins or arms and legs. **2.** the act of swimming: *a swim in the pool.* **swam, swum, swim ming**

swing 1. move back and forth with a steady motion: *The rope swings from the tree.* **2.** a seat in which you can move back and forth. **swung, swing ing; swings.**

T t

tad pole a very young frog or toad. **tad poles.**

tag[1] **1.** a small card fastened to something: *a price tag, a name tag.* **2.** follow closely: *Her little sister tagged along.* **tags; tagged, tag ging.**

tag[2] **1.** a children's game. **2.** tap with the hand: *She tagged me out.* **tagged, tag ging.**

tai lor a person whose business is making clothes. **tai lors.**

take **1.** lay hold of: *Take my hand to cross the street.* **2.** receive; get: *Take some cake.* **3.** use; make use of: *We took a train.* **4.** subtract: *If you take 10 from 20, you have 10.* **took, tak en, tak ing.**

teacher and class

teach er a person who teaches. **teach ers.**

team **1.** a group of people working or acting together. **2.** two or more horses or other animals hitched together. **teams.**

teeth **1.** more than one tooth. **2.** anything like teeth: *teeth of a comb.*

tell **1.** put into words; say: *Tell us a story.* **2.** know: *I can't tell who it is.* **3.** order; command: *I told you what do.* **told, tell ing.**

tem per a ture **1.** the amount of heat or cold in something: *The temperature today is ninety.* **2.** more heat in your body than usual: *He has a very high temperature.* **tem per a tures.**

ten one more than nine; 10. **tens.**

tent a shelter made of canvas or skins, held up by poles. **tents.**

tenth **1.** next after the ninth; 10th. **2.** one of 10 equal parts. **tenths.**

that *That* is used to point out some thing. We use *this* for the thing nearer us, and *that* for the thing farther away from us: *Shall we take this ball or that one?*

the a certain one: *The dog I saw had no tail.*

their of them; belonging to them: *They raised their heads as we passed. They like their new sister.*

a coil of **thick** rope

them the persons, animals, or things spoken or written about: *Call the girls and ask them to come along.*

then **1.** at that time: *It was colder then.* **2.** soon after: *The noise stopped and then began again.* **3.** next in time or place: *First comes summer, then fall.* **4.** in that case: *If he broke the dish, then he should clean it up.*

there **1.** at that place: *Sit there. There is my hat.* **2.** *There* is also used in sentences such as: *There are three houses on our street. Is there a store near here?*

they the persons, animals, things, or ideas spoken about: *I had three letters. Do you know where they are?*

they're they are.

thick **1.** far from one side to the opposite side; not thin: *This is a thick stone wall.* **2.** measuring from one side to the other: *This brick is two inches thick.* **3.** heavy like glue, not like water. **thick er, thick est.**

thing any object or material you can see, hear, touch, taste, or smell. **things.**

think **1.** have ideas; use the mind: *She will think about our problem.* **2.** believe without knowing: *Do you think it will rain?* **thought, think ing.**

third **1.** next after the second; 3rd. **2.** one of 3 equal parts. **thirds.**

this *This* is used to point out some one thing that is near. We often use *that* for the thing farther away from us and *this* for the thing near us: *This coat is mine. That one is yours.*

those *Those* is used to point out several persons or things: *Those are my sisters. Do you own those dogs? Those books are yours.*

three one more than two; 3: *Three and three make six.* **threes.**

three

time **1.** all the days and hours there have been or ever will be **2.** a way of counting time: *What time is it?* **3. times,** in arithmetic, means multiply or multiplied by: *2 times 10 is 20.* **times.**

tip[1] **1.** the end part: *The tip of her finger was cut.* **2.** a piece put on the end: *His cane has a rubber tip on it.* **tips.**

tip[2] **1.** slope; slant: *Look out, the boat is tipping.* **2.** turn over: *Don't tip your glass of milk.* **tipped, tip ping.**

to **1.** in the direction of: *Go to the right.* **2.** *To* is used with action words: *She likes to read. We had to jump over the puddle of water.* **3.** *To* is used to show action toward: *Give the book to him.*

too **1.** also: *The hikers are hungry and tired too.* **2.** more than enough: *You gave me too much.*

told See **tell.** *She told me. Has she told you?*

took See **take.** *Who took my book?*

tip[1] 1.

tool an instrument that helps you do work: *Dad carries his garden tools in a bag.* **tools.**

tooth **1.** one of the hard, white parts in the mouth, used for chewing. **2.** something like a tooth: *Each sharp point on the edge of a saw is a tooth.* **teeth.**

tooth brush a brush used for cleaning teeth. **tooth brush es.**

top[1] **1.** the highest part: *the top of your head.* **2.** the part that is up; the surface: *the top of the car, a table top.* **3.** the highest: *the top drawer, the top shelf.* **tops.**

top[2] a toy that spins. **tops.**

track 1. steel rails for trains to run on: *Be careful crossing the railroad track.* **2.** a mark left: *There were tire tracks in the snow.* **3.** a place where races are run. **tracks.**

train 1.

trade 1. getting something in return for giving something: *My kite for her bat was a fair trade.* **2.** make a trade: *Will you trade your candy bar for these peanuts?* **trades; trad ed, trad ing.**

train 1. a line of vehicles or cars that move together: *a freight train, a wagon train.* **2.** bring up; teach: *She trained her dog.* **trains; trained, train ing.**

trum pet a musical instrument that you play by blowing into it and pressing keys. **trum pets.**

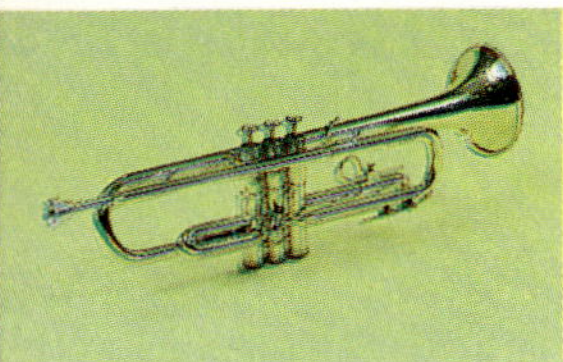

trumpet

try 1. set out to do something if you can: *He will try to build a car.* **2.** find out about: *Try this game.* **tries, tried, try ing.**

tu ba a musical instrument that you play by blowing into it and pressing keys. **tu bas.**

turn 1. move around a center as a wheel does: *The merry-go-round turned.* **2.** cause to move as a wheel does: *I turned the knob three times to open the safe.* **3.** a change of direction: *a turn to the left.* **4.** a chance to do something: *It is her turn to read.* **turned, turn ing; turns.**

tur tle neck a round, high, closely fitting collar on a shirt or sweater. **tur tle necks.**

two one more than one; 2. **twos.**

U u

un der 1. below; beneath: *The ball is under the table.* **2.** lower than: *He is under six feet tall.* **3.** less than: *Children under five years old go in free.*

up 1. to a higher place: *The bird flew up from the water.* **2.** to or at the top of: *He went up the hill.*

up on on. *Take the pot off the stove and put it upon the table.*

us the person speaking plus the persons spoken to or about: *Our teacher asked us to help her. The librarian told us a story.*

use 1. put to work; put into action: *We use our legs in walking.* **2.** lose or spend by using: *She used three sheets of paper for her poster.* **us es, used, us ing.**

V v

verb a name for certain kinds of words. In *He is my brother, is* is a verb; in *We danced at the party, danced* is a verb; in *Joe likes pizza, likes* is a verb. **verbs.**

ver y more than usual: *The wind is very cold.*

a **walk** in the woods

W w

wait 1. stop doing something or stay till something happens: *Let's wait for the bus.* **2.** the time of waiting: *I had a long wait for the plane.* **3.** be ready; look forward: *She is waiting for spring to come.* **wait ed, wait ing; waits.**

walk 1. go on foot: *Walk to the corner with me.* **2.** the act of walking: *We took the baby for a walk.* **walked, walk ing; walks.**

want **1.** wish for: *She wants some candy. Do you want to be an engineer?* **2.** need; be without. **want ed, want ing.**

was *He was a giant. I was late for dinner.*

wash clean with water: *Wash your doll's face.* **washed, wash ing.**

wa ter **1.** the liquid that fills the oceans, rivers, lakes, and ponds, and that falls from the sky as rain. **2.** sprinkle or wet with water: *The gardener waters the flowers.* **wa tered, wa ter ing.**

water 1.

way **1.** how to do something; how something is done or can be done: *Scientists are looking for ways to fight germs.* **2.** direction: *Go that way.* **3.** how to go. *Can you find your way home?* **ways.**

we the persons speaking: *We went riding.*

well[2]

wear **1.** have on the body: *Wear a coat today.* **2.** last long; give good service: *These shoes will wear well.* **wore, worn, wear ing.**

well[1] **1.** completely: *He knew the story well.* **2.** in good health: *She was sick, but now she is well.* **bet ter, best.**

well[2] a hole dug in the ground to get water or oil. **wells.**

went See **go.** *We went home early.*

were *We were late. Were you late? The children were picking flowers. The flowers were picked by the children.*

we're we are.

wet covered with water or other liquid; not dry: *Bring me a wet towel, please.* **wet ter, wet test.**

whale a sea animal shaped like a huge fish. **whales** or **whale.**

what **1.** *What* is used in asking questions such as: *What are you doing? What happened to him?* **2.** *What* is also used in sentences such as: *I don't know what she said.* **3.** *What* is often used to show surprise or other feelings: *What a ride!*

when 1. at what time: *When does the show begin?* **2.** at the time that: *Stop singing when the music stops.* **3.** at any time that: *We always laughed when the clown fell down.*

where 1. at what place: *Where is the money?* **2.** to what place: *Where are you taking them?* **3.** from what place: *Where did you get those shoes?*

which *Which* is used to ask about persons or things: *Which girl won the game? Which bicycle is yours?*

white 1. the color of snow, salt, or cotton. **2.** having this color: *Our house is white with a red roof.* **whit er, whit est.**

who *Who* is used in asking questions about persons: *Who is that?*

whole 1. having all its parts: *This is not the whole set of books.* **2.** in one piece: *Cut your sandwich; don't try to eat it whole.*

why for what reason: *Why did she bring two sandwiches?*

wil der ness a wild place; land with nobody or very few people living in it. **wil der ness es.**

will 1. be about to or going to do something: *She will start soon. I will go now.* **2.** be able to: *The boat will hold four people.* **would.**

win 1. succeed over others: *Our team will win the race.* **2.** get by work or by skill: *She won a prize for running.* **won, win ning.**

wind air that is moving. Wind can be strong or gentle. **winds.**

wish 1. need and hope to get something or for something to happen: *I wish I had a new bike.* **2.** something wanted or wished for: *Her wish for a friend came true.* **wished, wish ing; wish es.**

wind blowing a flag

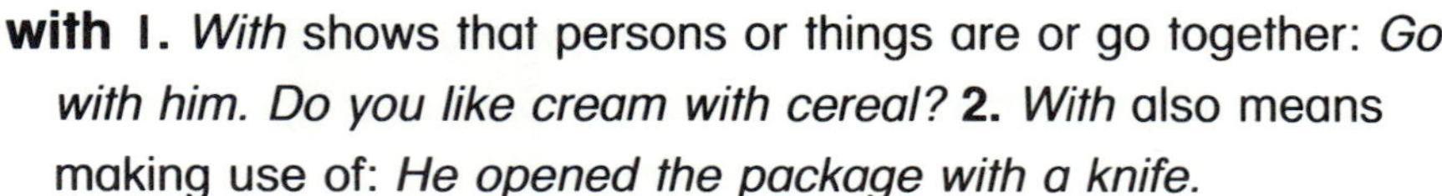

with **1.** *With* shows that persons or things are or go together: *Go with him. Do you like cream with cereal?* **2.** *With* also means making use of: *He opened the package with a knife.*

won See **win.** *This team won the game.*

word **1.** a sound or a group of sounds that has meaning: *I can't hear a word you are saying.* **2.** the writing that stands for a word: *Can you read that word?* **words.**

man at **work**

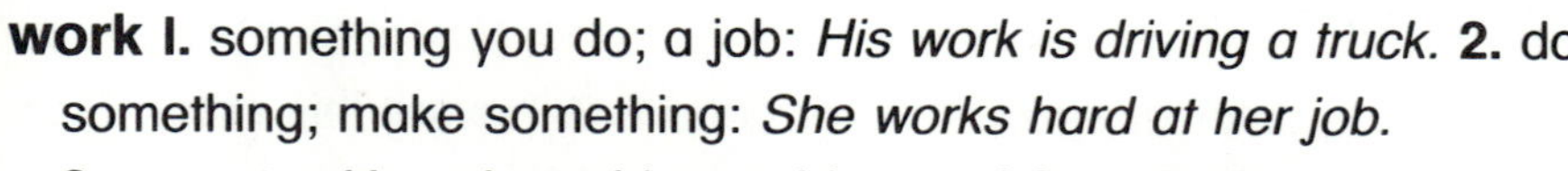

work **1.** something you do; a job: *His work is driving a truck.* **2.** do something; make something: *She works hard at her job.* **3.** operate: *How does this machine work?* **worked, work ing**

Y y

yel low **1.** the color of gold or butter. **2.** having the color of gold or butter: *a yellow flower.* **yel lows; yel low er, yel low est.**

yellow lemon

yes **1.** a word used to show that you agree. **2.** an answer that agrees: *The votes were three yeses and two noes.* **yes es.**

you the person or persons spoken to: *Are you there? I see both of you. I'll give you a book.*

your of you or belonging to you: *your head, your shoes.*

you're you are.

Z z

zig zag with short, sharp turns from one side to the other: *We traveled in a zigzag direction. The path ran zigzag up the hill.*

zoo a place where animals are kept and shown. **zoos.**

Handwriting Models

a b c d e f g h i

j k l m n o p q r

s t u v w x y z

A B C D E F G H I

J K L M N O P Q R

S T U V W X Y Z